Praise for *Irresistible Change*

"Phil Gilbert helped redefine how we thought about change at IBM—treating change like a product people chose to adopt, rather than a mandate to follow. *Irresistible Change* distills that approach into a powerful, practical playbook."

—Ginni Rometty
Former Chairman, President, and CEO of IBM,
and best-selling author of Good Power

"When embarking on a technology-related change at scale, it seems natural to get focused on the tech when success is actually about the people. They need an appetite and path to change the way they think and work. Phil's change-as-a-product mindset, experience, and stories can help anyone build a more effective approach to transformation, one that results in real, practical outcomes."

—Doug McMillon
President and CEO, Walmart

"*Irresistible Change* is Phil Gilbert's brilliantly insightful account of his time leading and driving IBM's move toward a new way of operating—nothing less than turning a battleship against headwinds and currents. His success was not serendipitous, but instead the product of thoughtful planning, careful communication, and relentless pursuit of doing what works. Less complicated than difficult, change demands deft, committed leadership, and a deep understanding of both the challenge and criticality of adapting."

—Stan McChrystal
General, US Army (Retired)
Founder and Chairman/CEO of McChrystal Group,
and best-selling author of Team of Teams

"The transformation of IBM into a design thinking organization is probably the most amazing corporate transformation in the history of American business. When Phil Gilbert came to Stanford I told him it was impossible—and I was dead wrong. Read this book to understand how he did it, and how you can make change irresistible."

—Bill Burnett
Executive Director of the Life Design Lab at Stanford University,
and best-selling author of Designing Your Life

"This is simultaneously the most radical and most pragmatic story of transformation you will come across anywhere. It would appear ridiculously ambitious to attempt to change the culture of a company the size of IBM and yet Phil Gilbert helps us truly understand what it takes to drive large-scale cultural change through design thinking. Anyone with similar ambition should take careful notes."

—Tim Brown
Chair Emeritus of IDEO,
and best-selling author of Change by Design

"In *Irresistible Change*, Phil Gilbert shares bold, carefully uncomfortable moves—like flying stakeholders in on a Sunday and banning laptops on Monday—to surface hidden resistance early. By designing for discomfort, he transforms skepticism into belief and makes lasting change truly irresistible."

—John Maeda
VP of Artificial Intelligence and Design, Microsoft Corporation,
and best-selling author of The Laws of Simplicity

IRRESISTIBLE CHANGE

IRRESISTIBLE CHANGE

A BLUEPRINT FOR EARNING
BUY-IN AND BREAKOUT SUCCESS

PHIL
GILBERT

WILEY

Library of Congress Cataloging-in-Publication Data is Available:

ISBN: 9781394367757 (Cloth)
ISBN: 9781394367764 (ePub)
ISBN: 9781394367771 (ePDF)

Cover Design: Ryan Caruthers
Printed and bound by CPI Group (UK) Ltd, Croydon, CR0 4YY
C9781394367757_131125

To my wife, Lisa, without whom I wouldn't have this life, this career, or this book. And to my late brother, Harry, who continues to inspire me to be better than I am.

Contents

Introduction: Transforming How Change Is Adopted

If ever there is a misnomer, it's *change management*. It rarely causes change and it's almost always mismanaged.

Why? The answer seems obvious to me: almost all leaders desiring change are businesspeople, but they never run their change initiatives like businesses.

Change should be regarded as a high-value-add product that deserves the same levels of resource support and operational rigor as any of your top-performing products. This means clear ownership, strategic leadership, and, above all, profit-and-loss accountability. Only when you treat change with this level of structure and discipline will you set it up for success.

In this model, change is your product, your organization is the marketplace, and its teams are your customers.

Change as a product must also be packaged and presented as a premium offering. No one values economy-class change. Only a platinum-tier solution will spark the excitement and customer demand required to drive widespread adoption of change, and have it stick.

That was my experience while leading IBM's global transformation. Beginning in 2012, my colleagues and I helped thousands of interdisciplinary teams at IBM become more entrepreneurial, more agile, and more customer-focused.

For all those 1,200 teams, we never had to mandate change, never had to beg anyone to join. In fact, we made the teams pay for our services. One-by-one, these 1,200 IBM project teams utterly transformed their way of working because the entire design and execution of the program was based on delighting them and adding value at every touchpoint.

Those changes have stuck; they've become the cultural core for how IBM does business today.

For IBM's global workforce of almost 400,000 people across 170 countries, we introduced radically different skills, practices, tools, and work environments. For another quarter million outside IBM, we provided learning tools and achievement certifications that enabled IBM clients to work more closely and productively with the company. Through Harvard Business School's executive education program, countless others have since received certificates informed by our original change program.

The business results have been astonishing. IBM reduced overall product time-to-market by 50 percent. The company reduced the average time project teams needed to align on initial requirements by 75 percent and cut the time required for product development and testing by one-third. Employee engagement soared across virtually every level of the company (which I felt was the program's most important strategic achievement). We created a program of *irresistible change*, one that people inside and outside IBM chose to opt into and benefit from.

Although it took us years to achieve these changes among the hundreds of thousands of IBM employees around the world, what made the crucial difference was the groundwork we laid in year one. During our third quarter, when we were still working with our first seven "customers," we could already see how our program was poised for self-sustaining long-term success.

All change is hard. Change at scale is even harder. But the hardest challenge of all is making change at scale that sticks. Looking back today, long after I and most of my original core team have moved on, I get the most satisfaction from knowing how profoundly our changes stuck and flourished at IBM. The new ways of working we introduced in 2012 have since become so deeply rooted in IBM culture that they now constitute IBM's everyday approach to product development, client service, and innovation.

About This Book

Hundreds of corporate executives and organization leaders outside IBM have asked me about the company's transformation over the years. My conversations with them have convinced me that this approach to change is unique and can help any organization, big or small, for-profit or non-profit, high-tech or low-tech, public sector or private sector, manufacturing or services. Most of the stories I've told these leaders appear in this book, and you have them to thank for the book itself. Without their persistent encouragement, I may have never bothered to commit all these stories to print.

The one through line you will see from beginning to end is how the program team thought and behaved like a startup leadership team. We accepted full responsibility for IBM's adoption of change and would have accepted its failure willingly if our market didn't value our product enough to pay for it. When problems arose, we didn't blame IBMers who "didn't get it," we blamed ourselves for failing them. If you can put together a change program team with that perspective and level of commitment, then it's game over.

I'm aware that books of this kind have certain limitations because every reader's circumstances are unique, and I can only speak of my own experiences. However, because of our common humanity, people and organizations all over the world experience the stages of change in very similar ways. In the book, I describe the universal experiences of any product or service and expand on that in the Appendix: The Irresistible Experiences Playbook. It is a reliable framework for designing your own change program. With adoption of change as your goal, you'll find that anticipating and fulfilling your stakeholders' needs across each of these contexts is a proven pathway to success.

Look at the Status Quo with Disdain

The present is far more fragile than we often realize. Technology is an ever-present disruptor that has a way of commoditizing what once felt unique, driving a kind of Moore's law–like acceleration into every corner of our daily workflows. Accepting this reality opens the door to a powerful truth: market leadership tomorrow will be determined by your ability to embrace and direct change today.

Change is inevitable—that much is clear. But what sets great organizations apart is the intentionality and speed with which they navigate change. Contentment with the way you work in the present is a setup for disaster in the future. A much healthier approach was once expressed to me this way: "We must always look at the status quo with disdain."

Organizations that adopt this mindset at scale in the coming years will be the true winners—in the marketplace, within their communities, and even on the battlefield. In every type of industry, companies must use this disdain for the status quo to cultivate cultures of curiosity, innovation, and adaptability. Over time, these organizations will develop something far more valuable and powerful: an institutional predisposition—almost an instinct—for provoking continuous meaningful change.

Through our change program, we rediscovered and unleashed an entrepreneurial spirit that had been buried at IBM over the decades. The goal of this book is to inspire others to learn from that experience—and to improve on it. Everything we achieved at IBM was just a prototype, a proof of concept for what comes next. What began more than a decade ago is now a sturdy template that I hope others will build on and make their own at any organization, of any size.

1

Setting the Stage

Never in my life had I imagined working at IBM. I launched my first software business in 1984, when I was just a few years out of college. For the next 25 years I was a serial software entrepreneur until 2010, when my third startup, Austin-based Lombardi Software, was bought by IBM. While the exit was great, it was a strange experience to be absorbed into IBM with my fellow 250 Lombardi employees. Until that time, IBM had been one of our fiercest competitors.

Lombardi's products were in the mundane middleware space of business process management (BPM). Our software performed similarly to BPM offerings from IBM, Oracle, and half a dozen other smaller competitors. And yet, Lombardi was winning the market. We did it the way any great company wins: we nurtured a culture that actively sought out ways to better solve our customers' problems, and we constantly investigated the latest technologies that might improve the user experience. Institutionally, we challenged ourselves to always look at the status quo with disdain. Our customers loved our software, loved us, and many of them working at major enterprises sang our praises and advocated for our products among their peers at other companies.

It was this reputation and our growing market share that led to the IBM acquisition, which made our investors happy and left me wondering what I'd do next. I committed myself to working at IBM for a year to help integrate Lombardi's operations but making a career at any big corporation never interested me. After my year at IBM was up, I imagined leaving in search of my next startup.

It took only about two months on the IBM campus in Austin to leave me feeling like I needed to get out sooner. The buildings reflected the distinctive corporate architecture of the 1970s and 1980s, with granite walls conveying the primacy of the institution and the insignificance of the individual. To an Apple fan like me, the campus felt a lot like the stereotype of IBM at the time. We had a nickname for the place: the insane asylum. In the hallways, we Lombardi folks were constantly getting scolded to "be quiet!"

At IBM, it seemed like creativity and passion were subordinate to conformity and fitting in.

The process of integrating an acquired company's technology into IBM is called *bluewash*. It entailed reviewing and rewriting much of Lombardi's computer code to conform with IBM standards. Admittedly, it's a necessary process to ensure compliance with all the legal, licensing, and security frameworks that a global company like IBM operates under, but it took longer than it needed to. And, frankly, it was as dreary and spirit-dampening as it sounds. The simple reality was that bluewash took a lively growing startup and inadvertently retrained its employees to adjust to IBM's slower, process-oriented culture. The result was an exodus of many of the startup's most entrepreneurial people.

In our case at Lombardi, bluewash was estimated to take about a year, and because everyone was busy rewriting our existing functionality in the IBM way, innovation was on hold. One of Lombardi's three main products in development at the time was a new software-as-a-service (SaaS) app for Apple's soon-to-be-released product—the iPad. However, a senior IBM executive overseeing our acquisition assured me with great confidence that "business-to-business SaaS is not going to be a thing." And so, just weeks before Apple's iPad was introduced to the world, our app was killed.

My spirit was also getting killed, but more slowly than the iPad app. I urged my team to find ways to get our bluewash completed in under six months because I didn't think I could last much longer. I said as much to Robert LeBlanc, the senior vice president at the top of our division, during a visit to IBM headquarters in Armonk, New York.

"Man, I look around and I just don't see where I fit," I told him over dinner. "I don't see the curiosity for delivering great software that people love to use and the execution behind it." From what I'd seen, IBM culture seemed to value maintaining the status quo above everything else. There were too many processes—with mindsets to match—that seemed built to stifle creativity and worked against satisfying the needs of our users.

"Seriously, no offense intended," I said. "If it's working keep doing it. It's just not my thing."

I noticed Robert wasn't smiling. But he wasn't pissed off either. And, while I didn't know it in the moment, what he said next would detour the course of my career for the coming decade.

"Why do you think we bought Lombardi?" he asked me. "You do things differently. We know we need to change, but we don't necessarily know how. So, I think you're looking at it all wrong. You're looking at people in roles that exist and processes that exist and you don't see yourself. I get it. But think about it like this: you think you know where we need to be? Then what can you do to help?"

I joked that I'd be glad to take over as CEO and start making some changes.

Robert had a better idea. He suggested putting me in charge of IBM's entire business process management group. If I took the job, Robert said, he wanted me to use my authority to change the group's culture so it was more like Lombardi's, and less like IBM's.

Changing [a Small Part of] IBM

It was an intriguing proposition. The BPM portfolio was a mess that needed some serious sorting, with 44 software products in various niches, many of which competed against each other. I would need to integrate Lombardi's products and people into this mix, along with those of another acquisition, a French company that had continued marketing its products under its original brand name for more than a year.

And although the BPM group was more than four times the size of Lombardi, it was tiny from the IBM perspective, with just 1,100 employees in a company of about 400,000. Running this walled-off sandbox meant I could make some radical changes to operations, and they would barely register as ripples within IBM. At the very least, I hoped, I might retain some of Lombardi's more spirited and valuable people.

Could it be done? I wasn't sure. Lombardi's company culture relied on a customer-focused work method called *design thinking*, which called for us to study how our users responded to our products. Then we iterated and tested prototypes with them. We knew these people intimately, we cared about their tasks and how easily they were able to perform them, and we designed each update with that as the priority. That's why our customers loved our products. Software development at Lombardi was flexible, fast, and based on human-centered problem-solving. It was miles away from IBM's hierarchical, procedure-oriented, engineering-centric work culture.

Could I take the BPM group culture from there toward the Lombardi direction? Would IBM people in the BPM group be willing to adopt a new way of working that was entrepreneurial and customer focused? I had no idea, but the prospect of working at global scale with a remit to build something great sounded like a fun way to stretch my entrepreneurial muscles. Robert had promised me free rein, a promise I was eager to put to the test. And if it didn't work out? Well, that fourth startup was always waiting for me somewhere out there.

The transformation of IBM's BPM group took 500 days. We pruned the bloated product line from 44 to 4. We reduced the head count from 1,100 to 700, and this included adding some new employees as professional designers to help guide the work of the product teams. Those 500 days involved a lot of rough sledding. Sacred cows were gutted amid org chart infighting galore. There were many days I figured I'd gone too far, and I expected to see an email from Robert with some version of "Stop! Enough already!" That email never came.

While the changes upset a lot of people, they inspired others and rallied them to the cause. I found allies who liked the new practices so much they wanted us to move even faster. The French company, in particular, had many folks who urged us to be much bolder in streamlining the product portfolio. And there was David Millen, a career IBMer who headed BPM engineering and had long been frustrated with IBM's slow pace and product infighting. Dave became an invaluable ally in getting buy-in from his fellow IBM veterans on the executive team and throughout the group.

I learned from him that there were, in fact, many IBMers who'd also felt impeded by the old culture and were thirsting for change.

Over the 500 days, we cut down product time to market, raised gross margins, and grew our market share in the BPM space. Our customers loved the new product line and our employees were engaged and energized. Robert, meanwhile, protected us and caught a lot of flak on our behalf—more than I knew, at the time. His forbearance of my sometimes heavy-handed ways (ham-handed, some might say!) had paid off.

Can We Do This Everywhere?

About this time, at the end of 2011, Ginni Rometty was seated as the ninth CEO in IBM's 101-year history. Although the company still reigned as the world's largest computer services provider, her immediate challenges included slowing sales growth and sagging employee morale. Ginni had worked her way to the top at IBM over 31 years, and although she loved IBM, she was intimately familiar with the root sources of the company's troubles: our clients didn't like using our products, it was difficult to do business with us, and we weren't moving fast enough. Ginni put the question to her top executives: what are we going to do?

That's when Robert offered a suggestion: "We have this guy in Austin. Maybe he can help."

Robert asked me to put together a presentation on the BPM group turnaround to share with members of IBM's top leadership teams at the senior vice president level—Ginni's direct reports. Over the next couple of months I took the presentation on the road in meetings with various leadership teams, and I told the BPM story over and over.

I opened my presentation recounting our outcomes in plain business terms: speed to market (faster), head count (down), revenues (up), profit margins (up), and market share (way up). Only after I'd gotten their attention with outcomes did I delve into the how of change and discuss the particulars of design thinking as a method for product teams to get better results faster.

These senior executives and their teams were impressed with what we'd accomplished but they were also skeptical in varying degrees that any of what we'd done could apply to their own areas. They saw that I had certain advantages as an outsider, stepping into a dysfunctional situation with a mandate to make waves and years of experience in this other way of working. They all saw the need for change, but few of them were eager to disrupt their own fiefdoms. They had deep, and not unreasonable, concerns: could this type of change be done at scale? And was I the right person to run it?

In those sessions (and also later with Ginni) I offered the same frank assessment of IBM culture that I'd given Robert many times before. Even when we were making visible progress in the BPM group, there were veterans of the IBM way of doing things who proved to be stubborn sources of obstruction. Yes, the BPM group had greatly expanded its market share, but it had done so in spite of IBM culture, not because of it.

When I told this to Ginni in our meeting, she took no offense. She seemed impatient to move the conversation toward some actionable result. "Okay," she said. "What can we do to have that happen everywhere at IBM?"

"I have no idea," I confessed. My direct line of authority as head of the BPM group seemed essential to what we'd accomplished there. How could I affect 400,000 people, none of whom reported to me? Further, many of the changes we'd made seemed obvious to me, intuitive, even. How, I wondered, could I scale intuition?

Ginni asked me to think it over and draft a plan for changing IBM's global culture.

I agreed to try. I admitted I didn't know the answer, "but I'll give it a go."

Back at the office in Austin I started mulling over Ginni's words. "What can we do to have that happen everywhere at IBM?"

I knew that a typical corporate response to a problem of this kind is to throw bodies at it. In this case, the thinking might be, "Gilbert sounds like a crackpot, but he's done some good things. Why not give him 50 people, mostly scrubs who are being underused anyway, and see what he can do? Give it a year or two and see if there's any impact." That's the normal ineffectual response. What would be a more desirable alternative?

I did some back-of-the-envelope math to estimate what our end goal might look like. In the product groups alone, there were so many thousands of engineers and product teams at IBM that I guessed we'd need to hire at least 1,000 new design professionals in order to make a transformative change in how IBM's work was done. To manage the change initiative, a small but full-time program team would be needed for recruitment and hiring, program support, and to develop IBM's own form of design thinking and related practices, one that could be implemented at scale throughout the company.

This was a lot. I wondered if it might be more than Ginni and Robert had bargained for. I could hear George Harrison's lyrics in my head, about how it takes patience, time, and a lot of money to do something right. Before I worked out any of the details regarding costs and timelines, I figured I'd better check to see if I was even in the ballpark of their expectations.

I emailed a very high-level spreadsheet filled with rough estimate numbers. "You may think the solution is 50 people, but it's not," I wrote. "It's more like a thousand. And it's not people we have that you can reassign. We'll need to hire 1,000 net new heads, because they have skills we don't have at IBM."

I explained also that in year one, we could only hire about 100 designers, because experience with that first cohort would teach us a lot about what to look for in the next round of hiring. All told, it would take five years to hire and deploy 1,000 design professionals to IBM teams. And that 1,000 would still be less than half the total designer head count needed to involve every IBM project team in this new way of work.

I knew Ginni might be disappointed to hear this. The need for change was urgent, and I was talking in terms of years, not to mention the cost of all this. But I knew firsthand it had taken us almost two years to turn around the culture inside the BPM group. Turning around IBM's culture across 170 countries would be so much more complex that I had to give proper respect to all the factors I knew I knew nothing about. Promising a two- or three-year timetable would have felt good to everyone, but it would also have been a setup for failure.

"Okay, got it," Ginni said. She promised to get back to me.

In less than a week I received word through Robert: "Go."

Me, on the phone: "Awesome. I'm on it!"

Me, in my head: "Oh, shit. I'm the dog that caught the bus."

Change Is an Offering, Not a Mandate

That was May 2012. I had about four months to architect the program and develop the financial plan that would be submitted for approval through IBM's fall plan budgeting process.

Here's how I worked through the problem. Culture change is hard, and most people resist it. That's a given. But when the status quo is failing, that's also hard. No one in IBM disputed the facts that Ginni laid out when she became CEO, yet no one came to work at IBM intending to create these outcomes. Nobody enjoys delivering crappy user experiences to their customers or shows up to work thinking, "I hope I can take longer than necessary to make decisions today." The senior IBM executive who completely misread the market for SaaS and killed our iPad app didn't do that because he wanted IBM to fail. He simply climbed the ladder of success in a narrow, blinkered culture that rewarded respect for the status quo.

That's what culture does to people. It's powerful. That's why culture change is so important, yet so hard.

I thought about all this and realized the problem IBM faced in achieving change was virtually identical to the kinds of problems I faced whenever one of my startups introduced a new product: how do we get people to change to something new when it seems easier to stay with what they've got?

The answer was always the same: you make it dramatically easier for them to solve their problem, and you improve the quality of their outcome. Product 101. So why not apply modern product practices to the challenge of launching a change program?

In order to lead change, you turn change itself into the product. You invite employees to buy in, and you lavish attention and resources on your earliest adopters. By framing change this way, *your organization is the market for the product and your organization's project teams are the potential customers for your new product offerings.*

Further, you don't mandate change, you offer change. People choose to adopt your "product" because it provides them a better work experience. You just have to make damn sure your offering creates recognizably better outcomes than the status quo.

This insight proved to be the central animating factor for everything that followed. It was what I called the *magic trick* of our entire transformation—how we got hundreds of thousands of people to embrace change of their own free will.

It also gave me the proper framework for conceptualizing how the plan would play out over time. I would serve at the head of a program office that would operate like any other product team. Our office would develop, market, and support a product called design thinking. In year one, we would obtain a few cross-functional project teams as customers committed to learn this new way of working. These first teams would apply design thinking practices, tools, and methods to real company projects. Our key performance indicators would be adoption rate, speed of work, and customer (the teams') feedback. Our value would be proven both by the adoption and engagement of the first teams, and, critically, also by whether we'd developed a pipeline of opportunities from future teams willing to pay to join the program.

I've talked to a lot of people about change over the years, and they tell me they've never heard of a plan for change framed in this way. Some assume the difference is explained by the unique nature of design thinking, and I set them straight. Design thinking was merely the kind of change that IBM needed most urgently in 2012; it was our *change provocation*. Your organization is likely to have a very different need for change today, but all that means is that you have a different change product to sell. Maybe the product is a reorganization or a quality engineering initiative. Maybe it's digital transformation, an artificial-intelligence-everywhere initiative, Agile adoption, or even a return-to-office initiative. You name it. Whatever change your entity needs, you can introduce that change by starting with a product mindset and by developing a product offering to be offered and sold into the marketplace that is your organization.

Conspicuously absent from the cost estimates in my plan were traditional training sessions that would educate masses of employees about design thinking. In fact, the plan had zero time allotted for generic training or presentations to anyone about the overall change agenda.

The objective of the program I proposed at IBM would be to help project teams do better work, one by one, using the new approach. Scaling the program would be measured solely by numbers of projects successfully working in this new way. To me this was critical: *the only education on design thinking would be presented to a full-time project team, in the context of that project, so that even the education session itself accelerated the expected business outcome.*

The project team, not the individual, should be the atomic unit of a change program. Teams, not individuals, deliver outcomes. This is the only place a change program can demonstrate tangible value.

Common sense, right? Therefore, if the business outcomes produced by project teams are truly all that matter, why hold workshops and trainings for individuals? In a similar vein, why would we ever provide generic workshops on design thinking? They might be fun and stimulating, but no generic workshop has ever produced a measurable business outcome.

In fact, delivering any change content outside the context of an ongoing team project will have at least three predictable results that are, at best, a waste of time and at worst downright destructive:

- People forget the material and don't change how they work. (This is the best possible result.)
- Or, worse, they project in their minds how this new learning may or may not apply to their projects, often arriving at mistaken conclusions that close their minds to real change.
- Or, worst of all, they find this new learning fascinating and eagerly attempt to apply it with their own teams. They do so without any expert advice, direction, or support. They screw it up and produce negative outcomes, which they then blame on the change initiative.

As far as I can see, there is simply no measurable benefit to training when it is held outside of a working relationship with a project team intent on producing positive outcomes. Those team members are inherently incented to win and will work through many barriers early change programs encounter, accelerating the perceived value of change across the organization.

A One-Year Runway

I went on to develop the budget details for the fall plan as though it were a five-year business plan for scaling design thinking among IBM's project teams. It read like a startup's pitch deck, with Robert as my intended investor because he'd agreed to house the program office within his division. Besides funding salary and overhead for myself and the program team, I budgeted year one dollars for the travel and program funds needed to run the first teams through the program, as well as for hiring the first 100 designers.

I requested funding only for year one. Like any venture capital plan, I showed the expected ongoing costs for the out years, but they weren't important to get perfect. That's because I knew that in reality, we had a one-year runway to prove our worth. If we did, then we'd raise a new round of funding for year two based on what we'd learned and how quickly we were expanding.

Also, and this is key, part of the change-as-product model requires that in those out years many of our operations would be paid for through sales. New, incoming teams must value our change product enough to pay for it out of their own budgets. The program office was like any startup. We had a one-year runway, and if the results weren't outstanding, there would be no money for year two and the effort would be scuttled. However, if we were successful, we could continue selling change to our marketplace.

That was the challenge we took on. Our aim was to provide a product that was so desirable it would be worth paying for. It would be, in a word, *irresistible.*

Remember, I'm not a trained designer. I wasn't schooled in organizational behavior. I'm a product guy. I've been making things and selling them to people since I was 11 years old. Taking a new product to market is hard; you're engaging customers who would prefer not to bother learning a new tool or deal with a new vendor. You need to demonstrate how your product benefits them in the specific ways that those users' value most, so much so that they feel it's worth the trouble of adopting something new and paying for the privilege. Anyone attempting cultural change, assuming they want meaningful change that will last, should have the same objective.

For years, that was our obsession at Lombardi. Our products offered better experiences for end users because Lombardi would have been dead if they didn't. Lombardi software had to be so good it would lure customers away from the comforts of giant brand names like IBM and Oracle. We needed customers to *change* when it would have been easier for them not to.

And, to bring that product mentality fully into frame, consider that building it and selling it is just the start. After the sale, you have to support the product and improve it continuously until your buyers become believers and enthusiastic advocates for what you sell.

A lot of what I knew about corporate change I had learned from John Kotter's classic book *Leading Change*, which emphasizes the vital importance of enlisting allies, removing barriers, and achieving short-term wins that show real progress. I'd internalized these and many other aspects of Kotter's teachings because they also reflect my everyday entrepreneurship experience. Kotter's diagnosis of the eight chief obstacles to change was evident in almost every challenge I faced while bringing new products to markets already cluttered with competitors.

What Kotter and most other change theorists overlook is the vital importance of accountability for the team that's leading change. Our metric for success was very clear when we started in 2013. If, after year one, no IBM teams wanted to pay for us to help them learn this new way of work, we would be out of business. How many change leadership teams have made that same high-stakes wager on their success?

As you'll see, that very clear metric—succeed or perish—prompted us to work much harder, and with much greater focus and imagination than if all that was expected of us was to fulfill workshop enrollment quotas. Everyone in the startup world knows that it takes tenacity and creative problem-solving every day in order to lure new customers away from the security of the status quo. Why not channel that same kind of powerful startup energy toward the even greater challenge of enticing comfortable employees to take up the mantel of change?

Cupcakes, Birthday Cakes, and Wedding Cakes

What we accomplished at IBM was unusual solely because we began from this premise of change as product, and each chapter of this book reveals an aspect of the architecture required for delivering culture change that directly follows from this premise.

I'm frequently asked "Okay, but what parts of this do I *really* have to do?" People point to their constrained budgets and want to know which program elements are essential and which ones can be dispensed with.

I would never claim this way of change is the only possible way forward (well, perhaps I would), but if you find it attractive, you must consider there is an integrated holistic design to it. If you want systemic change that sticks, you should resist the urge to pick and choose which parts of this program you like best and which ones you consider unnecessary. The program architecture is a lot like built architecture: removing one load-bearing beam can bring the whole thing down.

If you want to learn from the IBM example and lead change that sticks, what I've learned is that you need to do everything.

Start as small as you like, but cover every base on that reduced scale. You might start with just one project team and grow from there, the same way that a startup company might begin with a single small product and only one customer. You must do everything for that customer. You must support the customer fully, build references, earn their product endorsements, and trumpet the news of that customer's success with the product. You must believe in change enough to see such ongoing support as an investment in your company's future.

At IBM we used a metaphor when working against product release deadlines: "cupcakes, birthday cakes, and wedding cakes." Leading up to a product release, there is always a development phase when time to market (and cost) must be traded off against desired functionality. The most important thing in such a circumstance is to make those trade-offs in ways that ensure the final product still offers a complete and delightful user experience.

We talked about the long-term vision for the product as being a wedding cake, a beautiful vision that we aim to deliver over time. But right now, we may only be able to deliver a birthday cake. And more likely, in an agile world, we may need to deliver a very fast cupcake. But that cupcake should be one perfect and delicious cupcake that meets everyone's expectations for what makes a great cupcake. That's how to build a loyal user base that might someday have the appetite for the full wedding cake.

Cupcake thinking helps avoid the temptation of making the most expedient cuts to functionality, just to get the product out the door. Do that and you risk putting out a product that doesn't really hang together. Instead of that perfect little cupcake, you've delivered slices of half-baked wedding cake that no one wants.

For your change program, that's the outcome to avoid. If you start with a modest cupcake-sized program, for one team designed to hit all the bases and demonstrate improved outcomes, you'll earn the resources and time to bake a fine birthday cake next. But if you overreach and launch the program with a poorly made lopsided wedding cake, the experience will leave a bad taste in everyone's mouths, and your change initiative may never recover.

Even if you start small, if you do it right there is no end to its scalability. From our own cupcake beginnings we would grow year by year, from team to team, business unit to business unit until the wedding cake was in place. Across product, human resources, finance, the information technology group, and every other division, IBM achieved a level of cultural transformation that, back in 2012, we would have regarded as unthinkable. We'd done it everywhere.

Go Time

As the fall plan process churned along, I didn't let the enormity of the task bother me. I wasn't certain it would happen, despite the verbal sign-off from Ginni and Robert, which, at the time, felt more like a spiritual commitment. The formal budget process had its own mysteries. Would their spiritual currency see the project through to real-world dollars? And what would I do if they said yes, but without full funding?

I put these questions out of my mind and went about thinking about the team members I needed. My desired core leadership team fell into place quickly and I started connecting with them and other potential allies inside the company. I told them what was ahead, and that if funding was actually secured, I'd be asking them to join my team. Each one said they'd be glad to do it.

And then, to my mild surprise (and to the credit of Ginni, Robert, and many other supportive top execs) the fall plan was approved for 2013 as submitted, funded in full, down to the penny. We were off and running.

Takeaways

- **Change is a product, not a mandate:** Transform your initiative into a desirable offering that teams choose to adopt rather than an edict they're forced to follow. Your organization is the market, and every project team is a potential customer who must be convinced that your approach will solve their problems better than the status quo. This product-centered mindset creates voluntary adoption that spreads organically.
- **Teams are the atomic unit of change:** Focus exclusively on working with complete project teams rather than training individuals or running generic workshops. Only intact teams deliver measurable business outcomes that prove your value, and team-based learning ensures new practices are applied immediately to real work rather than being forgotten or misapplied.
- **Start with a perfect cupcake, not a half-baked wedding cake:** Begin with a comprehensive but small-scale implementation that demonstrates every element of your approach working in harmony. A complete, satisfying experience for a few teams builds more credibility than a partial, disappointing experience for many. As with any product, the early days are about proving product-market fit, not proving scale.

2

Branding
the Program

When I took on the task of change at IBM, I was a novice at working at scale, real scale. Global scale. I wasn't even a novice. I was pretty much an idiot.

I learned the hard way that when you introduce the idea of change to a large organization, there are as many views on what needs to change as there are listeners. Whatever the specific nature, or *provocation*, of change (e.g. design, Agile, reengineering, reorganization, return to office) every individual in your audience will perceive your message through the lenses of their own preconceived notions.

During that first summer of 2012, I got my first inklings of how easily this dynamic could put our change program at risk before it started. When I gave my presentation to IBM's annual Technical Leadership Summit at our Research Triangle Park campus in North Carolina, it drew an unexpectedly wide variety of negative reactions.

I'd been eager to meet this group of IBM's 250-plus most senior and respected engineers because I wanted to identify a handful who could be critical to our success. I attended the summit with Charlie Hill, a British-born designer who held a master of arts degree from the prestigious Royal College of Art. While he had a storied past working on iconic design teams prior to joining IBM, 15 years earlier, he also held engineering degrees from leading UK universities and had been appointed one of IBM's Distinguished Engineers. If there were gaps in understanding the connection between engineering and design, I counted on Charlie to help me explain.

But during our presentation, we could see audience members rolling their eyes. Afterward, the reflexive dismissals came pouring out.

"Oh, we already do this."

"We already know what we need to build."

"We don't need new people to be involved in our decisions. They'll just slow things down if we have to explain things to them."

Charlie and I expected to encounter a lot of skeptics in this crowd, but we also hoped to find a few eager supporters. We found none. Aside from the occasional kind words of interest, we came up against a wall of negativity. Even among those who acknowledged Ginni's call for change, many dug in their heels to debate the merits of design thinking as an appropriate response. Either they disputed its effectiveness without understanding it, or they cited their past experiences with design thinking done badly. These senior engineers wanted Charlie and me to know they had their own way of doing things and had no interest in changing. If IBM needed to change, they said, those changes were needed elsewhere in the organization.

Throughout that summer, as I visited IBM offices around the United States seeking candidates for our first project teams, the drumbeat of close-minded objections never stopped. I returned from the road convinced that the word *design* was a serious problem. Everyone had a fixed opinion of what design was, and how design thinking functioned ("It's a workshop"). The terms *design* and *design thinking* were saddled with so much baggage that they were consistent sources of needless distraction.

And there were grains of truth, of course, in the objections. Design thinking can be done poorly, just like anything. But no one wanted to engage us in a constructive conversation about how to do this new thing well. I suspected that people feeling threatened by change knew they couldn't dispute the need for change head-on, so shooting arrows at the type of change we were promoting was the safer way to counter the threat.

I needed to change the subject. I wondered what I could do to steer future discussions toward the thing that really mattered: improving team performance.

A complicating factor was that I *had* met dozens of IBM employees who, despite an obvious lack of skill, were calling themselves designers. They also claimed their teams were using design thinking to work through their problems. Even on cursory review, though, it was clear that the work these teams were doing wasn't good. If people thought I was huckstering this type of change, they weren't wrong to question it. I didn't want *anyone* to observe the mediocre performances of these self-proclaimed designers or their teams and assume that's what we were after.

I thought about this and saw how easy it was to assign yourself a title, like "Designer," and to deliver mediocrity or worse. So, I became concerned that once we got going and showed positive results, imitators would arise. And then, when those teams underperformed, their managers would use their failure as a knock on the entire program. I was fine taking my lumps for anything I or my team screwed up, but we couldn't survive counterfeit versions of execution reflecting poorly on the idea of the overall program.

An idea is interesting. It unlocks thinking. But execution is key. Perhaps 90 percent of the value of an idea is derived from its successful execution. We needed a system to easily distinguish the "real" teams—those who were sanctioned by and working with my program team, executing at the highest levels—from everyone else in the organization.

A Brand You Can Trust

Generally speaking, I don't enjoy discussing design in hypothetical terms or in isolation from the outcomes design can contribute to. What we'd achieved in the business process management group had been done by understanding project problems using new design thinking tools and then solving those problems using an *integration of new and existing methods*. The teams thrived by using hybrid approaches appropriate for each specific project. A new culture isn't borne from whole cloth; in fact, the stickiness of change will be determined based on how well the new is integrated with the parts of the existing culture that are worth keeping. It will be an 80/20 thing: you'll only adjust perhaps 20 percent of the behaviors, but it will be the 80 percent most highly leveraged part of what emerges.

While thinking through all this—the poor quality of existing design efforts, the likelihood of counterfeits, and the need to reflect the "integrated new" versus just "design"—it hit me that our product needed a name. If we were going to drive the adoption of change with a product approach, our product would need a suitable brand name that would define us in the marketplace.

A brand you could trust, infused with our unique set of values, practices, and expectations. It made sense. Given that our program was its own thing (and not a generic design training program) then we should *name* the thing.

As it turned out, all those cranky senior engineers with their misgivings about design thinking had done me a tremendous favor. They forced me to face what's been well-known about buyer behavior for more than 100 years. Buyers respond to brands, not products. You can make a valuable thing, but without brand marketing that communicates its value, buyers will likely ignore it. Look at the humble-but-handy laundry detergent tablet. It's been around since the 1960s but never gained much sales traction until the 2010s, when Procter & Gamble launched the Tide Pod. Today the P&G Tide Pod dominates a $3 billion market—because they named the thing.

By giving this thing its own brand name, we could put some space between our mission and all the wrong-headed notions about design and design thinking that were swimming in our colleagues' heads.

What's in a Name?

To choose the ideal brand name for change at IBM, we needed to identify a name strong enough to travel the globe with a minimum amount of unwanted baggage. We needed a name that would encompass everything important about our change initiative, so we ruled out including words such as *design* or *design thinking*. We were more than that, and the name needed to reflect as much.

We had to take stock of the values we would want that name to represent. Initially, I considered the potential benefits of a name that might confer a sense of company continuity and familiarity. Perhaps it should invoke IBM's nickname, and we could call our project teams Big Blue teams. But the risk would be that while dropping the baggage associated with "design," we'd be taking on some new Blue-colored baggage instead. Maybe people are tired of hearing about Big Blue. What if some old-timers recoil at misusing the name, as though we were trying to put new wine in old bottles. Some might be offended by an upstart office appropriating the hallowed Blue nickname. "Wait a minute. Aren't all our project teams a part of Big Blue?"

There was another brand value that was much more compelling than continuity: that of exclusivity. The highest value products in any marketplace are the ones that have cachet. Think about Louis Vuitton or Rolex. People opt into these brands because of their reputations for high quality and limited availability. That's the same brand reputation we wanted for our change program.

Essential to making change irresistible is the perception that a team's admission into the change program is a badge of distinction and achievement. We would be starting out with a limited number of teams, and we needed to attract a lot of project leaders willing to compete for those few slots. Having far too many applicants would provide us with the opportunity to review the applications critically and ensure we were working only with teams that were highly motivated to learn these new and unfamiliar practices. Competition amid scarcity would also enable us to choose a good mix of project team types.

What kind of name would reliably and unambiguously convey that feeling of status and exclusivity? We'd want a brand name that would make the members of our accepted teams feel proud they'd been admitted. And it would be a name with no baggage, no past associations, no prior significance within the organization.

We ran some names through searches on the IBM intranet to rule out words already in use for employee awards and honors. The list narrowed from there. For a while we considered the word *Signature*, but we settled on *Hallmark*.

As we saw it, *Hallmark* was the perfect blank-slate word. A hallmark is a sign of distinction, nothing more, nothing less. It's simple to spell and easy to say. Within IBM, the one thing you'd know about teams with the Hallmark designation is that they had been specially chosen through a competitive process for an ambitious project aimed at changing IBM's future trajectory. That's all anyone needed to know. These are teams of distinction, and if you want your team among them, just fill out the Hallmark application form.

Hallmark was a neutral shiny vessel into which we could pour the values of the Hallmark program and its teams. In the same way that you can't separate the glamour of Jane Birkin from the limited edition Hermès Birkin bag, we would attempt to fuse the many positive existing elements of IBM's culture with the new provocations that our program brought to create something new, valuable, and desirable. Hallmark stood for more than design and design thinking; it would stand for everything else needed to deliver great outcomes, too. Hallmark would become the gold standard for how teams worked at IBM.

Looking back, I can't believe I didn't see this from the start. The product approach to creating irresistible change depends on having a memorable brand, no different from any other product. In fact, if I had it to do over, I would have named our office the Hallmark Program Office on day one, just for the sake of brand consistency.

Defining the Brand

An important and immediate benefit of having the Hallmark name was that it gave me a much-needed point of focus whenever I had to communicate the rules and responsibilities for teams to be admitted into the change program. Under the Hallmark name, it was easier to communicate the underlying values of user-centricity without getting into the weeds debating features and functions of design. Branding our program offered the advantage of discussing it on its own unique terms of culture and values. Under the Hallmark banner, the program would represent a higher aspiration than the implementation of design thinking. The cultural priorities Hallmark represented would be clear.

This unlocked a new, more powerful way for me to tell the story. I remember addressing a town hall that summer and speaking in my customary informal way about our plans. Later that day, when I sat with a group of site leaders for a question-and-answer session, I was shocked by how their questions expressed mistaken assumptions about what I'd said earlier. Some of them "quoted" me in ways that completely misconstrued my meaning. As I attempted to set them straight, in the back of my mind I imagined what all the other people in the town hall had made of what I'd said. Were those people now passing on their mistaken assumptions to others, who in turn were misunderstanding them and acting on them?

But when I began speaking of Hallmark values, I avoided these kinds of problems. We all want our leaders' words to turn quickly into action. That behavior is at the root of organizational effectiveness and efficiency, but only if those words are carefully chosen and properly understood. If you can keep the conversation on values and the program's intention, it's more difficult to be misconstrued than when you assert specifics about, say, design or program implementation, which may not be universally applicable to every situation.

This is a particular discipline of change communication that the Hallmark brand facilitated. Change leaders often dive straight into discussing only the new methods and processes, overlooking the value in existing culture. This both alienates those who built that culture and ignores the real-world context where changes must be integrated. Moreover, technical teams often assume they understand these new concepts through their own experiential lens, leading to costly misunderstandings and lost momentum.

Don't get me wrong—I enjoy sharing ideas and discussing all the tools and techniques that went into our work. I loved our designers and the work that they were doing and was very involved with the team responsible for our design thinking practices. I would spend hours with them. But getting into conversations with the broader community at IBM about such things was unlikely to reflect Hallmark's intention and advance the cause of change.

It's akin to praising your product's features, as opposed to promoting benefits in terms of brand values. You probably love your product's features but they're all about the factual *what* of change. When you speak more to the emotional *why* of change, to your values and aspirational intentions, people will respond with their hearts as well as their heads. The why message is more inspiring, more memorable, and is more likely to move people to action for change.

Protecting the Brand

Every premium brand name needs to be protected so it is only used in contexts controlled by the brand owner. For Hallmark, this meant that all our program team members and designers were instructed to decline discussing the work of any IBM project team that wasn't enrolled in the Hallmark program. Personally, I pretty much declined to discuss the particulars of design thinking with any IBM project team leaders that were interested in applying to Hallmark. I urged them to look at our introductory deck and work with our staff on the application process.

Why was I so cautious? Mainly, I knew our program was bound to arouse curiosity among other IBMers who were looking for a few tips they could take back to their teams. And while everyone likes to be helpful to their colleagues, I could foresee how my very informal assistance to any outside team could end up sullying Hallmark's reputation. What if, in six months, they release some costly crap software that fails to sell? That team leader might find Hallmark's past input to be a convenient excuse.

"Well, we tried the use some Hallmark training materials and I even talked to Gilbert for an hour on how to bring in designers for the project. But it all went sideways fast, and I won't make that mistake again. From what I've seen, this design thing seems overrated." I knew how convenient it would be to shift the blame over to "what the Hallmark people said we should do."

I was also concerned that the project teams we didn't accept into the Hallmark program might go ahead and hire their own design specialists anyway. Then they'd ask Hallmark's advice on implementation. Could we possibly share some of our training materials? Could we run a quick virtual workshop? I would have to say no.

You might wonder if I was ignoring the upside potential. Wouldn't these requests for help result in more Hallmark allies and help change happen faster? The reality is that someone who tries to do change on their own, without having the experts who are deeply involved in the integration of the specific new and existing methodologies that your program will deliver, will likely fail.

That's why I shielded my team ruthlessly against any scope creep from non-Hallmark projects. To my mind, we were a tiny office on a giant transformation mission, and we had no time or resources to spare. I even told Ginni and Robert, "I love IBM and I want IBM to be successful everywhere, but I can't care about anything but Hallmark now. I don't professionally care about anything that's not in this program." We were far too important to IBM's cultural disruption to have our own work disrupted along the way.

Setting this clear boundary gave us a layer of insulation from everything else going on at IBM. It gave me and the rest of the team a tremendous degree of focus. I know that sometimes your job is to be among the all-hands-on-deck during crises of one kind or another. It comes with the territory of most senior corporate jobs. But if the change leader is called away to help out elsewhere, I believe it can put the whole change program at risk. Change is about looking to the future, and you have to protect that at all costs; fire drills are inherently reacting to the old culture and the change leader should be divorced from that.

This is why you must uphold brand exclusivity and maintain the discipline of working only with the branded change teams you supervise. Otherwise, you can very rapidly become a victim of your success. It happens in a predictable pattern. The change program starts out very cleanly, as a few early change teams earn some quick wins and recognition from the top. The word gets out, and suddenly people come out of the woodwork wanting some of that goodness. Some have sincere interest in change and are allies, but others are merely ambitious and want to be associated with success. They're reading the tea leaves, and they want to be seen as a part of whatever has earned the CEO's favorable attention.

The change leader in this scenario, being a good corporate citizen, agrees to work with these independent teams, advise them, and share resources. The change leader knows full well that this is not the best way to do it. These ad hoc late entries to the change program have entered midstream and lack the onboarding and other ideal initial conditions for effecting change; it spreads your resources too thin. But when the leader doesn't have a brand framework to defend, it's difficult in corporate culture to reject friendly requests for help and advice. Inevitably, these ad hoc additions will fail to achieve the expected results, and any negativity and failure attached to them sticks to the change program's reputation. The advice given them by the change program had no shortage of good ideas, but failure was always likely due to flawed execution.

A parallel problem affecting change programs in most large organizations is that of duplicated efforts. More than once, people in the Design Program Office would discover a product team in some corner of the organization attempting to solve the same problem that one of our Hallmark teams were already working on. Trying to be helpful, they recommended that we extend our work to the duplicate team, incorporating its members into our Hallmark team. I always refused. I wanted us to work only with the team that qualified for admission to Hallmark, had gone through our onboarding, and whose management chain was in the loop. That other team working on the same problem could go its own way.

We had to stick to our simple and direct Hallmark brand promise: we recruit qualified project teams into the Hallmark program, we set them up in every way to win, and then we work with them until they win. We can't attempt to fix every problem we run into across this vast organization, as it would compromise our probability of solving the one problem we're attacking.

Learning to say no is an important leadership skill in general, but in leading change it is absolutely essential. Every change program is understaffed and underfunded, while on a mission to change the destiny of the organization. Without focus, you don't stand a chance.

At Apple's 1997 developer's conference, Steve Jobs explained his controversial decision to kill numerous projects on his return. His message was simple: focus requires saying no.

"And you know the hardest thing is, when you think about focusing, right?" Jobs said. "You think, well, focusing is saying yes. No. Focusing is about saying no, and you've got to say no, no, no. And when you say no, you piss off people."

Building the Brand

In large organizations, the real sign of power within the system is the size of your footprint. If you have a large enough head count associated with your program (whether they report to you or not), you have power. And power within the organization gives you the ability to achieve your goals faster.

This is another benefit of branding your change program. It gives you a way to establish "footprint" well beyond the few folks who you directly manage. Always be thinking about how to establish the biggest branded footprint possible, then market your brand relentlessly. As the Hallmark program grew in footprint size and power, the brand bolstered our success in more ways than we could count. Having a consistent label and definition under our control was essential in aligning our communications and rallying people around a common mission.

Change needs power. Assuming that the success of the change program is vital to the future of your organization, every move you make should involve growing the power of your brand. I'm not talking about power as power trip; I'm talking about the power to be bold, to take risks. Being able to ask for, and receive, resources of increasing scale.

As teams began to experience the usefulness of our approach, the perception of Hallmark as a premium brand inside of IBM grew rapidly, which is why in subsequent years we never suffered from a shortage of applications for admission. In marketing lingo, Hallmark prospered from what is called "the country club effect." Once we named the thing and then didn't allow everyone in, everyone wanted in!

Exclusivity increased our brand appeal among the top-performing teams in our marketplace, and, in turn, the strength of those teams helped burnish the Hallmark brand. Maintaining that dynamic helped give Hallmark the power to make change irresistible at IBM, and make it stick.

In retrospect, I don't know how we could have achieved that without the benefit of Hallmark's branding power. That's why, when I consult with companies, I recommend they gather all their disparate change teams under the supervision of a single program office with a distinctive brand name umbrella. I know of companies with a half-dozen new teams working within a formal Agile change program, while other project teams are simultaneously experimenting with their own aligned but somewhat different change provocation, like artificial intelligence. While it's true that all these seemingly disparate efforts may have used different technologies, they all represented a common change agenda from a values perspective and should be presented that way. These disparate efforts with different names are not only confusing to the organization, they squander the power potential of a common brand.

The Hallmark brand provided a sense of consistency, weight, and scale to what otherwise might have appeared to be a scattered group of unconnected projects and events. It unified the understanding of projects as diverse as a product team's mainframe software update to an HR team's rethinking the annual employee review experience. In all our communications, Hallmark served as a convenient shorthand in showing how change was happening steadily and broadly. As the number of Hallmark projects grew in year two and year three, they spanned an ever-greater number of user groups, technologies, and problem spaces. Their one common thread was that under the Hallmark brand, they were all executing a new way of work and driving a common culture change agenda.

With time, we developed a management system that was indexed on growing the number of Hallmark teams, so we could easily demonstrate the rising adoption rate of the new way of working. We established quarterly reporting that tracked each executive's Hallmark footprint—including team count, head count, budget impact, and geographic reach. This transparency sparked healthy competition among our executives, turning peer pressure into a powerful engine for change.

Throughout the organization, we were able to communicate a consistent story of IBM's ongoing adoption of change. Even the many IBM people who knew almost none of the specifics of what we'd been doing perceived Hallmark as a premium brand and Hallmark teams as accomplished and special. It was this brand halo that helped provide our little program office with the power we needed to make change at IBM irresistible.

Takeaways

- **Brand change as a premium product:** Create a distinct brand identity for your change program to distinguish it from other corporate initiatives; infuse it with values that make it desirable, even coveted. Your brand should become shorthand for excellence, making teams proud to be associated with it while helping you bypass the baggage associated with generic terms like *transformation* or *Agile* or *design thinking*.
- **Use your brand to magnify influence:** Exclusive, premium branding across disparate projects increases the change program's organizational footprint and perceived power. This also creates a "country club effect" where exclusivity drives demand and creates a high-status opportunity that ambitious teams want to pursue.
- **Avoid counterfeits; only work with branded originals:** Learn to say no to projects and requests that fall outside your branded program, even when saying yes seems easier or more collegial. Diluting your resources across ad hoc implementations will compromise both results and reputation, undermining your premium status. Remember Steve Jobs's wisdom: focusing isn't about saying yes, it's about saying no.

3

Designing the Leadership Team

The Hallmark program was set to launch at the start of 2013 with funding guaranteed only for year one. Our tight timeline realistically meant that how we set up the program's initial conditions would be the difference between failure and success. With one shot to get it right, a lot was riding on the choices I made with our program's architecture. I needed to set a clear mission and assemble the right people in the right roles to execute that mission.

Like many change leaders, I'd assumed my remit was to achieve better outcomes by introducing a new capability—in this case the specific change provocation of design and design thinking. I'd led the business process management (BPM) group's turnaround thanks in large part to this and now I'd accepted the challenge of achieving similar results across all of IBM.

I'd been noodling on a mission statement along the lines of "bringing design back into IBM." Something like that. But it didn't fully capture the desired impact of change we needed to be successful. It was too small of an idea. Many of the changes within the BPM group went beyond just design and design thinking. They were also skills; change skeptics could easily put them in a box and dismiss them as a fad, an obstacle to serious engineering, an un-IBM alien "other."

31

It also nagged at me that the BPM product teams were under my direct authority, which would not be the case with Hallmark. The scale of Hallmark's ambition was enormous: *change across all of IBM*. I needed to understand and articulate how introducing this new way of working would matter more broadly than to just a narrow community interested in Design with a capital *D*.

I spent part of 2012 visiting with various companies to meet their designers and see what was working, and not working, for them. What surprised me most on those trips was the consistently high quality of the design teams I met with. In fact, the quality of the design teams at design-forward companies didn't strike me as being very much superior to design teams at companies I regarded as design laggards. There was a stark difference, however, in how the *non-designers* at those companies spoke about their design teams. At the design-forward companies, there was a level of respect for design among non-designers, something I didn't experience when visiting the design laggards.

Later, I'd come across a similar observation in a blog post by a product designer at Apple. The writer credited Apple's non-designers as the real heroes in driving Apple's amazing user-centered outcomes. Apple's secret was that everyone in the organization respected design so highly that they supported Apple's top-flight designers and allowed them to do their best work. The writer's point was that Apple delivers great user experiences not just because it has great designers but because Apple has a great design *culture*.

I realized that this was perhaps the crucial difference: Those cultures that successfully exploit an attribute are those that *value* the attribute, not those that simply *contain* the attribute.

In order to stick, a change provocation—be it design or Agile or artificial intelligence (AI), or the next big thing, whatever—must become *a coveted value of everyone in the organization*, and not simply a skill that some people have.

All of this meant that we would need to focus as much, if not more, attention on getting the culture to embrace the values of great design than we would on attracting designers to execute on it. Most efforts get this backwards. They spend more time on the mechanics of the change provocation and relatively little time on the cultural assimilation of the values behind the provocation.

At those design-laggard companies I'd visited in 2012, I saw the results when top skills are exercised without a corresponding culture change: excellent design teams do work that is marginalized or ignored by the non-designers in charge.

I suddenly saw that the real work of change was much larger than I had anticipated. When I started the change conversation with Ginni and Robert, I had to swallow hard when I estimated that we would need to hire 1,000 new designers over five years. Now I understood that for the new way of work to flourish at IBM, we also needed to get hundreds of thousands of non-designers to embrace and adopt these new practices as something clearly better than the old way.

The mission statement we settled on reflected this objective:

The mission of the Hallmark program is to
create a sustainable culture
of design and design thinking at IBM.

This signaled clearly that we were in the culture business, not just the design business. It was bigger than design, just as any change initiative needs to be bigger than the change provocation. It was no longer about who *they were* in design, it was about who *we are* as IBM. All of this meant that our program architecture needed to be built on valuing design—figuratively infecting everyone's DNA—not merely inserting design skills into our workforce. All our most costly activities—hiring designers, developing instructional materials, delivering training—would go to waste if we didn't instill a broader values-based foundation for IBM's new capabilities.

Consider how this formulation might apply to other kinds of change. If you make it your mission to create a sustainable culture of agility, then in addition to the tactical adjustments Agile requires, your program will focus on getting all the non-practitioners to align their mindsets with the principles of working though agile thinking. Too often, an Agile organization is anything but agile, if you get my drift. This focus on culture will require your program to advance the mission through all the levers of cultural influence within the organization—leadership, communications, and the many systems of record that reinforce particular practices. Elevating a culture of agility in all of these areas would be so much more impactful and sustainable than if you were to merely educate a number of teams in Agile practices.

In a similar way, working toward a culture that systematically accepts and embraces AI's disruptive potential will have far greater impact than merely offering AI skills training or partnering on an AI implementation. With AI in particular, training and implementation in the absence of culture change can be highly problematic. Many people have good reasons to resist AI, fearing it might have negative effects on their careers, the organization, or even on society as a whole. Addressing these fears head on (by communicating and acting on the values behind your AI rollout) will likely prove more important to the long-term success of the change program than training on how to use a new AI bot.

Not since the mainstream adoption of the internet in the 1990s has there been a more powerful transformational force than AI. And, as with the internet, how organizations adapt to this new technology will shape their priorities and cultural values for years to come. Programs that introduce AI need to be intentionally run as culture change programs so that the new way of working with AI embraces a future in which AI is inevitable, but aligned with your organization's long-term values.

Seeking Virality

All the choices we made from this point forward reflected the crucial relationship between design (our *change provocation*) and our culture (the values and default behaviors of an IBMer). It's hard to convey what an enormous task this felt like at the time. To put it in perspective: for every 100 designers we'd add at IBM, we needed to somehow influence about 5,000 others, having each of them adopt new values that would drive interdisciplinary teaming, empathy, and all the rest.

What would that mean for Hallmark's program architecture and our initial program conditions? What was the relationship between the new values we were introducing and the existing values as practiced? And because values and behaviors are not things *learned*—they're things *adopted*—how could we possibly make this impact on the organization's non-designers quickly and at scale? We needed changes to be inserted at almost the molecular level of the company's value system. We needed culture change at IBM to *go viral*.

Which begged the very question: how would we create a virus?

Few things in nature provoke change as fast as a virus. Viruses spread by infecting cells with new genetic information that changes them into virus-making factories. The newly manufactured viral bodies then flood the bloodstream and change other cells into virus factories, too. That's how viruses spread so fast. They create self-sustaining change at scale.

In a sense, the chief obstacle to bodily viral infection is similar to the obstacle faced by all change programs: host bodies are highly resistant to new information. In the case of viruses like COVID-19, its genetic information (called the genome) needs to be smuggled into the cell interior. The COVID-19 genome rides inside a protective protein casing called a *capsid*, which is covered with protein spikes capable of adhering to a host cell. These protein spikes have evolved to pair with protein receptors on the host cell exterior, enabling the virus to attach and deliver its genomic information (see Figure 3.1).

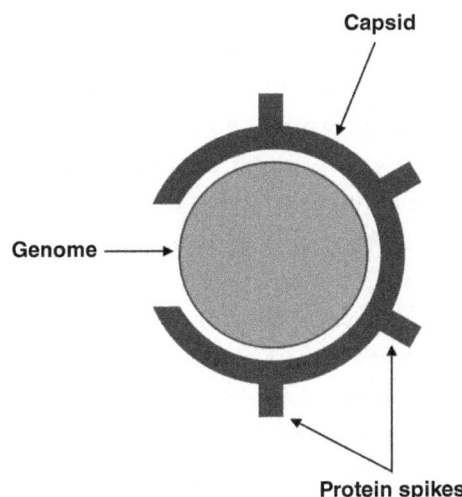

Figure 3.1 Structural anatomy of a virus particle (virion).

The protein capsid and its spikes have three functions:

- Protect the genome.
- Interact with the host.
- Deliver the genome's information.

Protect, interact, and deliver also happens to be the function of any effective change program office. With the newfound clarity of mission—wholesale culture change—we'd somewhat unwittingly stumbled on the conclusion that Hallmark's program architecture would be most effective if we designed it like a virus.

In the virus model, the genome is very much like the change program's content, which contains information for transforming the host body's functions. I was fortunate to have Charlie Hill (my co-presenter at the Technical Leadership Summit described in Chapter 1) as Hallmark's Chief Technical Officer. He brought credibility to the idea that good design was compatible with good engineering and other development practices like Agile. Adam Cutler filled the role of design practices leader. If Charlie was focused on those critical non-designers, Adam was squarely focused on the designers. These two were responsible for training all the new designers we'd need in year one, as well as coaching and monitoring the IBM teams selected for our program.

Despite their high level of professionalism and expertise, Charlie, Adam, and the whole design team would be introducing alien information likely to be resisted by the host organism's existing hierarchy, systems, and processes. These had been built over decades to protect and maintain the status quo. Presentations on design thinking would never have the power to crack those defenses.

So, in addition to the essential technical design leadership team, the job required a second team of leaders to take up the virus roles of protective capsid and attaching protein spikes.

This mental model prompted us to take stock of the systemic rejections our program would likely be subject to. We began by identifying the key points of failure commonly observed when change programs lose momentum and die:

- **Senior leadership** will withdraw their support for the change if they don't see steady, scalable progress toward desired outcomes.

- **Teams** will lose faith in change and become demoralized if management and the systems around them hinder their ability to sustainably adopt the new ways of work.
- **Individuals** will resist changing how they work if their adoption of new behaviors goes unrewarded by systems that aren't designed to recognize or reinforce them. They will also resist change if the benefits and opportunities don't appear relevant to their daily lives or the effort appears to lose steam.

The virus model helped us anticipate the program responses needed to protect our culture change mission. It showed where our architecture needed an interface—a figurative protein spike—to help our change genome infect IBM's culture.

For each of these common points of failure, the Hallmark program architecture called for one or more skilled business professionals—all with IBM experience and with strong preexisting IBM relationships:

- A Hallmark program leader (myself) to manage expectations among senior leadership
- A talent professional working directly with IBM's human resources (HR) office to introduce desired new behaviors into IBM's system of job descriptions, performance reviews, and career ladders
- A business systems professional to engage with the functions of the IBM chief financial officer (CFO) and chief information officer (CIO) on behalf of Hallmark teams, assisting teams applying to the program, and managing expectations among wait-listed teams
- A communications professional from the ranks of IBM's communications apparatus to help the program team promote our successes and sustain interest in the program (see Figure 3.2)

In the Hallmark program architecture, all four of these areas were aimed at supporting the core domain expertise of the design thinking and agile program.

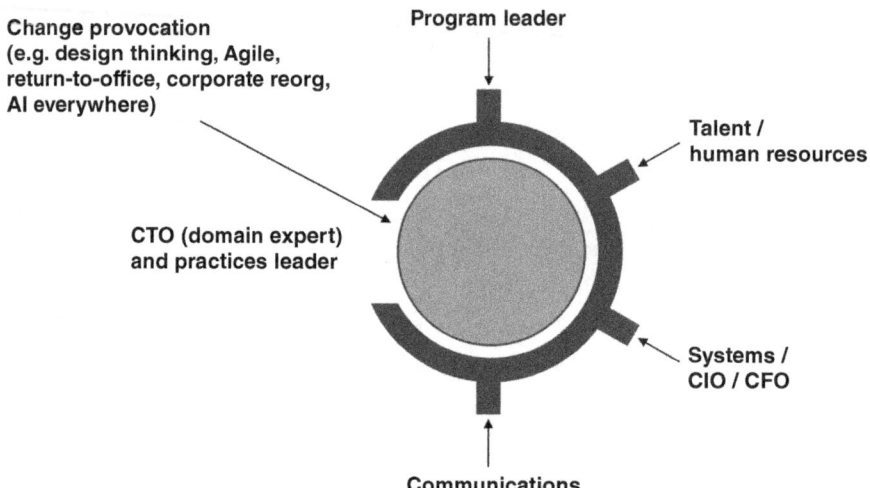

Figure 3.2   Conceptual model and roles of the change program office leadership team; designed to deliver, spread, and nurture a new *change provocation* into the host organization.

The Protein Spikes of the Hallmark Program Office

When assembling the leadership team for any change program, I'd suggest you make it a priority to assess each individual for their *attachment* capabilities. Top leaders on the program team need to be people the organization will be highly receptive to working with. In the best cases, they are familiar faces within the company who know how to get things done inside the existing culture.

Everyone on my team was dedicated to do whatever it would take to ensure that IBM's dominant culture wouldn't prevent change from taking hold. Initially, this meant working within the system, obtaining exceptions to rules so that Hallmark teams could do their work. But it also meant working to change those rules for all, which was the long-term goal. In essence, my leadership team was tasked with smuggling our new set of cultural behaviors into IBM's processes and systems, using the tactical successes of each Hallmark project as the proof for why this should be done.

The Program Leader

A successful product manager is often a good candidate for heading a change program, not only because "change is product" but also because such a person will bring credibility to the role in the eyes of senior leadership. This is someone accustomed to making the ongoing trade-offs and optimizations required of an in-market product, who understands business results, deals with budgets, and has a track record of inspiring and motivating direct reports.

I'm describing myself as humbly as possible, but for reasons I'll make clear, these truly are the essential competencies of a change program leader.

When I was first announced as head of IBM's Design Program Office (the formal title of the Hallmark program team) there was some grousing among design professionals that a non-designer should not be given such an important job. If the mission of the change program had been limited to inserting design skills into a business unit, I might agree with them. But as I've discussed, the change product is so much more than the change provocation.

The primary role of the program leader is to be a proxy of the senior business leadership in driving change and obtaining cooperation from the rest of the organization so that it scales rapidly. For that reason, this person's skill set should be associated with driving outcomes, not mandating inputs. In fact, it's probably best that the leader *not* be closely associated with the new thing at all.

However, change programs commonly leave this critical leadership role to the same person who is the content leader, even if that content leader has no prior experience running a business unit. When dealing with business leaders inside the organization, content leaders can come off as too dogmatic in their convictions about how their area of expertise should be valued. That tends to invite skepticism within the management ranks.

Business leadership, unlike technical leadership, requires a more balanced sense of spending priorities. My ability to express enthusiasm for both design *and* the bottom line proved to be an important source of rapport during meetings with senior leadership. As someone who also had profit-and-loss responsibilities, I could see eye to eye with the general managers heading IBM business units. While we may have had disagreements about investment from time to time, they appreciated that we shared bottom-line accountability.

Hollywood producers like to tell directors, "Make sure the money's on the screen." Raising money is hard and producers want to see where the money they raised made a difference. That's how I feel about this work. I want to spend money that makes a visible difference this week or this month, so we can show progress. This meant that I often chose "good-enough" options that allowed us to spend across competing priorities. I think this way because I know it's how a business runs, and the product of culture change is like any other business product. To stay the course in product development, senior leadership needs to constantly see what they're paying for. They want to see it all on the screen.

Content leaders, however, are more like movie directors. They want to get their craft right, and care less about cost. There's a famous story about the making of *The Godfather* when Francis Ford Coppola insisted on spending more than $10,000 on the Godfather's antique office desk. Then he hired a cinematographer who shot the movie's opening office scene in such moody shadows that Marlon Brando might as well have been sitting behind a cardboard box. The producers almost had a stroke when they saw the scene. It wasn't wrong to buy that desk, but in the early days of change, one rarely has the cachet of Francis Ford Coppola or the money of a Hollywood production!

With our one-year runway, we didn't have the luxury of *narrow perfection*, we needed *broad better*. Although design was the critical lever in our change, the design aesthetic, while important, was only one of many variables we needed to deliver to show the cultural impact we were aiming for. The program leader must have the perspective of the broader goals and be able to make the difficult trade-offs based on what constitutes "good enough."

The Talent Leader

To make change irresistible, promising career paths need to be laid out that will excite interest in the new thing. When people know that they are learning new skills that will be suitably rewarded, you can rely on employee self-interest to help drive adoption of the new way of working. Many change programs overlook the talent function entirely, relying on HR to somehow magically amend their systems to accommodate the new thing, or simply bypass these critical processes altogether. Every change program needs a talent function. Like every other aspect of change, you need someone dedicated to understanding where existing systems reinforce old behaviors and can influence new ones.

I brought in Fahad Osmani, with whom I'd worked for many years before I'd joined IBM. Fahad and I had a shared understanding of the type of culture we wanted to create. Initially, Fahad would play a critical role in establishing the entrepreneurial culture we needed inside the Hallmark teams. As he did this, he came to understand the hopes and fears of not only the new designers but also the non-designers who had become so critical to our understanding of success. Then, his more strategic function would be to help translate those learnings into the scalable ways our corporate HR systems and processes needed to change to reinforce the new behaviors we wanted. This is critical to making change stick.

I had always seen IBM's complex HR processes mainly as sources of obstruction and frustration, but Fahad helped me understand how those systems, properly hacked, would accelerate our success. He and Jodi Cutler, one of his team members, took up the task of integrating the values behind design thinking and Agile into HR's complex system of staff, manager, and executive job classifications, across design and non-design roles. It took many patient discussions with HR to update job titles, career paths, and incentive programs to get these new skill sets recognized in HR's systems of record. The work my talent team did was often tedious, but the end result was that IBMers who invested in change felt their enthusiasm would be rewarded in performance evaluations, while even those not initially bought into all this were able to see for the first time how their careers might be accelerated if they jumped on board.

The Systems Leader

At the outset of the program, I asked one of the product managers from the BPM team to join me at Hallmark and help with strategy and systems. Pierre-Henri Clouin (PH) quickly became essential to our success by generating interest in our product across IBM. He reached out to different teams, showed them what was possible, managed our potential "customer" pipeline, and brought new teams into the Hallmark program. A crucial part of his role was building strong relationships with the CFOs of each business unit. These connections helped ensure everyone understood the financial implications of joining Hallmark. His organizational expertise also made him the perfect liaison to the CIO office when Hallmark teams needed new tools.

When you're trying to change how people work, you almost always need to update their existing tools. However, this creates a challenge: organizations have invested heavily in making their current tools secure and stable. They're naturally hesitant to approve new tools, and when they do, the procurement, security, and customization process can take a very long time. This slow pace conflicts directly with the speed needed for an effective change program.

Oftentimes, business owners will go behind the information technology (IT) department's back, creating what's called *shadow IT*. While it's expedient, they actually work against themselves because by its very nature shadow IT applications are hidden from the scalable CIO organization. What seems like a short-term win is often a long-term loss for the organization because the CIO doesn't have the forward visibility into what the business needs and wants, or the why behind it.

We solved this problem by being overly transparent with our CIO office, gaining approval for a two-step strategy to bring in new tools. The first step was an ability to gain approval and set guardrails for the immediate use of pilot technologies by the Hallmark teams. For example, one guardrail might allow use of a new cloud-based tool, but with an agreement as to what types of artifacts could be stored—only those that weren't deemed confidential. Yes, this was manually administered, but our employees were trusted to make the right decisions. This was critical not only for getting the new tools in but it also sent a signal that Hallmark teams were getting access to the latest technology, further enhancing Hallmark's brand reputation.

The second step was the long-term interaction with the CIO, giving them visibility into the pilot use and access to the users to understand the tools' differentiation and importance. While many tools were piloted and rejected by the teams, many others were adopted and the CIO provided critical scale to that adoption, as you'll see in Chapter 5.

Having a role that nurtures these back-office functions is crucial to creating the conditions for irresistible change. That's where scale happens.

The Communications Leader

I could have easily overlooked the role of communications leader, but Robert LeBlanc assured me we'd need expert help delivering our message internally throughout IBM. He sent me to meet with his division's head of communications, Melissa Sader, and we ended up sharing Melissa's time each week (described more fully in Chapter 6). As a long-time IBMer, Melissa knew how to access all the various channels of communication that reached IBM employees and knew the critical people across IBM's large communications team. Every change program needs a communications liaison like Melissa, who had credibility among her peers in the organization so she could gain their cooperation when we needed it.

Hacking Culture to Change Culture

If there's one thing you take away from this book, I hope it's this: at every critical decision point, *the change program must be architected on the mission of sustained cultural adoption of the thing—as opposed to improving immediate competency in the thing.* Improving competency is a subset of the actual challenge.

New knowledge alone never has the power to shift a company's direction by even a single degree. Meaningful change is achieved only through an ongoing dialogue with the existing culture. We needed this small group of skilled leaders to understand how IBM's existing culture (systems, processes, behaviors) reinforced its old self, and in doing so could then instigate the hacks required for it to reinforce its *new* self.

A lot of the work necessary to achieve this is barely visible and doesn't look like "change," because it's about adapting the seemingly minor and arcane innards of the organization. But like the butterfly flapping its wings in China, small changes to the initial conditions in these highly scaled systems can have outsized impact.

When you look at the range of issues we surfaced and dealt with every day, it's easy to see how the culture change mission makes the program's scope so much larger than the competency being inserted at its core. For any new thing to have a chance at survival, these key roles need to be in place in order to properly influence all the systems surrounding the new thing.

Every Friday I assembled this group for our only regular standing meeting. We reviewed the week's events, reported emerging issues, and focused on tactical problem-solving. Personnel issues were passed along, tooling and systems were discussed or previewed, communication opportunities were raised, and if anyone had problems that required help from senior management, I took them up. When the design team ran into organizational obstacles, they could hand it off to the appropriate peer. For example, if someone in management above one of the Hallmark teams started interfering with how the team was working, then either PH or

I would get involved, which would free Charlie and Adam up to get back to working with the new teams.

It went the other way, too. For example, once Fahad got HR to change their systems to reinforce the adoption of design thinking skills, it would be Charlie and Adam who would connect with HR and provide the details of what needed to be in place. This would occur time and again, whether helping PH communicate something to a CFO, or Melissa who might be opening the door to a senior exec or an external analyst or reporter.

If we were going to bring the virus of design thinking into the very bloodstream of IBM culture, we understood that every member of the program team needed to be relentless change agents for every important function of the company. Every mission critical process and system of the company would need to be changed—sometimes in a big way, more often in subtle-but-difficult-to-achieve ways.

None of this is unique to design. It's how all change goes viral, becomes irresistible, and achieves scale. Companies that pursue change the other way—for example, by hiring consultants to train thousands of people to be certified in the new thing—will likely find that that within six months none of the teams involved are working any differently than they had been before. In one such instance involving Agile, none of the systems and processes of the central organization changed at all, so old behaviors were rewarded no differently than the new ones. With zero incentives for anyone to change, Agile in this case never had a chance to catch on, much less go viral.

Compare that with another common but faulty approach to change: the independent "innovation lab" or "innovation team" that goes off to solve a company problem in completely new ways, sheltered entirely from the existing company rules and culture. These teams return triumphantly with novel solutions and products to show off, demonstrating how the company could do great things if only people could work outside the bounds of its restrictive culture.

But these solutions are rarely adopted by the company and usually make no impact at all. They are intended to serve an inspirational function, but because their mode of work bears no resemblance to the existing culture, they offer no practical avenue for being replicated. Many times, those teams' members go back to their old jobs, and they're not expected to continue the new practices. Even folks who would like to follow the innovation team's example find it impossible, because none of the systems and processes in their everyday world has changed to support them.

These innovation teams gain a lot of attention because they often have dramatic outcomes to brag about, but they are incapable of changing the culture at scale. Real culture change in its early stages is subtle and incremental. It only becomes dramatic at scale.

What You Think Is the Work Is Not the Work

Working change through the systems requires tenacity. Working it through the humans requires grit. I never had any doubt that the initial IBM teams exposed to design thinking would like it and take it up gladly. They would be handpicked, no doubt, and work with us willingly.

What I didn't know was whether the positive experiences of these early teams would be impactful enough to begin to infect IBM culture. A lot of this depended on the designers we assigned to these teams. We needed them to be much more than highly skilled design professionals. We needed them to have the desire and mental fortitude to become valued teammates who could help initiate non-designers into IBM's new design culture.

Our first cohort of 65 newly hired designers arrived in Austin in summer 2013 for an intensive 90-day designers' camp. Nearly all of them were recruited straight out of some of the best undergraduate and graduate design programs in the United States, but we weren't there to teach them about design. Instead, our objective was to prepare them for their added roles as cultural ambassadors and to acclimate them to IBM work culture. As early-career designers, they would be exposed to technical languages they'd never heard before and business practices they'd never experienced before. We also wanted to prepare them for certain IBMers' indifference (or outright hostility) to the design skill set they'd been studying for years. We knew they would encounter engineers with decades of domain expertise who would be loath to see the balance of power shift inside their teams.

During the designers' camp I told them, "What you think is the work is not the work." That got their attention. "You think the work you're about to engage in is about design. You're wrong. That's what you studied. That's what you love. That's who you are. That's what you're passionate about and what you want to do. That's not the work. The work is everything you're going to have to do to get your designs implemented. And many times, this will be in the face of open resistance."

I explained that design within their Hallmark team would call on them to refine all their soft skills of empathy, collaboration, and teamwork. Getting to know their teammates. Learning how to advocate for their point of view, but also learning when to compromise in the name of "better," even if not yet "perfect."

In our program of irresistible change, the job of a designer included developing the communication and leadership skills necessary to get their ideas across in an engaging way. I told them how I'd met corporate designers over the years who complained bitterly that their non-designer teammates, "just don't get it!" In our program, it's the designer's job to inspire in their non-design teammates the desire to "get it."

"The most successful designers in the world are the ones that master all these non-design domains," I said. "This is the 'work' I'm talking about. Because it's hard, it's probably not something you've trained for, or that you'll enjoy doing." By the way, this goes for the new competency in any change program. The experts in the new skills must accept responsibility for the hard work of change—as opposed to the much easier task of delivering on their skills.

I told these young designers that to thrive as designers at IBM, "it will take backbones of steel." Our hope was that the designers would use these 90 days to develop an *esprit de corps*. I wanted them to build professional and personal bonds so deep that they could lean on each other for support on days that went poorly.

One late afternoon during the second week of designers' camp, I stopped by as a session was wrapping up at 5:00 p.m. In that moment, there was a rapid exodus of all the designers out of the building. No one hung back to talk with the instructors or linger to talk with each other. They just rose from their seats and left. It was so strange that I made a point of coming back the next day just before 5:00 p.m. It happened again. *Everyone*, it seemed, just rose from their seats and took off. It was as though a factory whistle had gone off.

This bothered me immensely. There seemed to be no healthy tension or nervousness in anyone, nor any meaningful bonds between them, other than, perhaps, a "see ya tomorrow" that I'd hear. I got more upset the more I thought about it.

Over the weekend, I wrote my team a somewhat intemperate email demanding we meet in my office at 7:30 a.m. on Monday morning. "I am not happy with the demands being placed on the campers," I wrote. "They are not being challenged; they are leaving early; and I believe we are failing them." I wanted everyone in this meeting to get clear on my expectations: "*I am certain in the campers' ability to respond; I am not certain in our ability to lead.*"

On Monday morning I asked them all, "What is happening here?!?" To my mind we had just 90 days to impress on these young people the difficulty of our mission—*their mission*. If we failed to make them ready, they would be chewed up and spit out by the Hallmark teams they were assigned to. It was our responsibility to not let that happen! We had to prepare them for the very heavy lifting they were on the front lines to do for us. Providing some happy-go-lucky experience—letting them just all punch out at 5:00 p.m. each day—was an abrogation of that responsibility. As I spoke, I grew more and more outraged.

Then one of the camp's designer instructors (I'll call her Carol) rose to her feet and said she was the likely source of the trouble. She showed me a slide from her day one opening presentation. It showed a clock with hand set at 5:00 p.m. announcing the end of each workday. Carol said she'd been emphasizing the importance of work-life balance in the design profession.

I thought my head might explode. I went off on the whole team. "This is NOT a 9-to-5 job! In fact, I want these people to *want* to be at work from 8-to-8 if they need to! They need to know that that's what it will take for us to win!"

Everyone got the message and left my office to prepare for the day's sessions. At the end of that day, which stretched well beyond 5:00 p.m., Carol came by my office to tell me she had resigned. She assured me she had no hard feelings, but added, "You need lions, and I'm a kitten."

It was, to my mind, one of the bravest and most honest things anyone who's ever worked with me has done. I remember Carol fondly for it. But she was right.

Irresistible change requires lions.

Takeaways

- **Culture thwarts competency every time:** Transformation is inherently a cultural problem, not merely a technical one. The *change provocation* (whether design thinking, Agile, return to office, whatever) is just the catalyst for deeper systemic change. Success depends not simply on how well people understand the new *change provocation* but also on how thoroughly the organization's systems and processes reinforce it.
- **Design your team to spread a virus, not just deliver a skill:** Along with experts in the particular *change provocation,* include leaders who have the skills and credibility to embed changes into critical organizational systems and processes. This dual structure mimics a virus, with content specialists providing the transformative "genome" while systems specialists create the "protein spikes" that attach to the organization's existing processes where change can be smuggled.
- **Change requires tenacity and grit:** The team guiding transformation must possess extraordinary resilience, emotional intelligence, and strategic patience, similar to a successful startup's leadership. As we discovered, this work demands lions, not kittens.

4

Selecting the First Projects

IBM was about to hire so many new designers that I decided to visit some of the top design schools in the country to let the deans and professors know what we were up to. On the Stanford University campus, home to the Hasso Plattner School of Design (informally called the d.school), I met with Bill Burnett who was running the undergraduate and graduate design programs, and David Kelley, a Stanford professor who founded both the d.school and the groundbreaking design firm IDEO.

I'd known of David since the 1980s, and it was his work and that of Alan Cooper that inspired my journey to design and design thinking. At that time, I was running a small Los Angeles software company that was breaking ground building software for lawyers and other professionals who weren't necessarily ready for computers on their desks.

My development team was proficient in getting the software to work technically, but as founder and CEO, it fell to me to ensure that it solved users' problems in satisfying ways. My days were spent selling our product and running the business. Each night I was sweating the details of the user experience, responding in my head to all the objections I'd encountered during sales calls.

When I first ran across the software design practices advocated by David and Alan, it blew my mind. I'd never thought about applying formal design practices to software; if I'd thought about it at all, design would have been about objects like Tandberg tape decks or the Eames chair. But applying formal design practices and professional designers to make better software? It was such an exciting insight that it started me on a decades-long journey of using design practices to scale product quality at pace, and even to build whole organizations based on the discipline.

Now more than 20 years later, as I'm telling Bill and David about IBM's plans to hire 1,000 designers over the next five years, I noticed that Bill was listening intently, while David seemed preoccupied. He was scrolling through email on his iPhone. IBM. Design. Didn't really click.

Finally, something I said about changing IBM culture caught his ear. He interjected wearily, "Phil, just remember, it's not as hard as you think. To change a population, you only have to win 25 percent of the people. That's the tipping point."

Before I could say a word, he paused and then blurted, "Wait a minute. At IBM, 25 percent is 100,000 people."

That was enough to get David engaged in the conversation. As we talked, I realized I hadn't considered the size of our task in tipping point terms. Even 100,000 was still a lot of folks, but as a new design point for us to aim at, the number felt more manageable.

Triggering the Right Response

On my office whiteboard wall I've got this quote by Nathan Shedroff, founder of the Design MBA program at California College of the Arts: "Design is about making choices that trigger the right response." I love that definition of design, and I use it often as a frame for my decision-making (although I'm sure I've mangled the phrasing—apologies, Nathan).

It helped me clarify the criteria for choosing our initial set of project teams to work with. First, I had to envision what was the "right response" we wanted to trigger. The ideal response would be teams from all across IBM competing for admission into the Hallmark program, and being willing to pay for the privilege. The people who could make that happen were the general managers (GMs). They controlled the operational purse strings required to pull the trigger.

IBM culture had long favored a high degree of decentralized decision-making power. The GMs in charge of individual business units within each company division pretty much set the rules for how their units ran. On the plus side, this told me that these managers had the budgetary leeway to support their teams in the Hallmark program if they were convinced it was worth it. On the negative side, this freedom gave GMs a streak of independence, accompanied by skepticism about whether something that worked elsewhere would also work for them.

Our challenge, then, was to provide evidence to these leaders that results from prior Hallmark teams were replicable by their teams. Our project selection process should be carried out with the specific intention of providing that kind of evidence.

It highlighted to me that the "right responses," or outcomes, were different for the program than for each team in the program. My outcomes needed to be behavioral and organizational and while they would be influenced by the project outcomes of the teams, the organizational response would be affected by other factors, as well.

If all we were interested in was having successful early teams, it would have been much easier to start out by working only inside Robert's software products division. But with the newfound clarity of what evidence would be needed to provoke the "right response" from those GMs and their inconsistent operations, we needed to spread out the first projects among several of IBM's 11 divisions. The added benefit was that it would also give the program immediate breadth and ensured that more of Ginni's leadership team would be involved and engaged in the change effort. "It can't all be me," Robert said.

Determining Our Capacity

We had to take a hard look at Hallmark's capacity for running the initial projects to determine how many teams—and how much of that organizational evidence—we could manage in year one.

Each project team would need one week of bootcamp-style in-person instruction in design thinking practices and tools. The teams would then need one or more new, full-time designers recruited and onboarded to work with them Additionally, each team would be temporarily assigned experts from Hallmark who would offer ad hoc support for a period of three to six months to help ensure the new behaviors stuck.

It sounds simple, but I knew we were taking a learn-by-doing approach that involved a lot of work beyond traditional training. During the one-week introductory bootcamp, we intended to work with each team on their project, demonstrating that the new way of working achieves outcomes meaningful to them. We weren't interested in "teaching" design, or "enabling" design thinking and Agile. We wanted every team member to experience how these practices helped them achieve better outcomes faster, so that by the end of the week they'd be on the path to adoption.

I wanted these initial project teams to feel the same excitement I had felt when I first encountered design thinking years earlier. I knew that once team members started moving faster and making higher quality choices, taking days to break through obstacles that had lingered previously for weeks or months, they'd never want to go back to the old way of doing things. Generic design thinking workshops couldn't possibly achieve the levels of engagement and learning that we would achieve with team members using design thinking to ideate and collaborate on their own work.

But doing the week-long instructional program this way would also be a lot of work. Our program delivery people would need to provide each project team with materials tailored specifically to that team's project. Preparing these would require that my team spend many hours investigating the specifics of each project and adapting terms and artifacts to the specifics of the incoming team's real-world work.

Given our program team size and funding levels, we estimated that our maximum capacity for all this work would cover approximately seven Hallmark teams. Taking on more than seven in year one would risk leaving us spread too thin if any of the projects needed more attention than we expected.

At the same time, we couldn't play it safe and do fewer than seven. As it was, the number seven got some resistance from Robert and Ginni for being too small. There were at that time perhaps 3,000 or more teams working on projects at IBM. How could we possibly make a difference with only seven in our year one? Yet, that was my decision. First and foremost, each team in the program needed to be staffed to win, and overwhelming force was preferred over just squeaking by.

We also needed a manageable number of teams in year one so we could spend the time learning how the new practices worked in various settings. We'd sacrifice numbers in year one so that we were ready to scale much faster in year two and more quickly move toward that 25 percent tipping point. Also, seven teams could still involve a large number of people, because many IBM teams included dozens or even hundreds of people across multiple countries.

Seven is by no means a magical number for starting with this change model. The number of initial teams you deploy is dependent on your budget, the expertise you can tap, and the size of your organization. Regardless of organizational size, however, it is critical to start with multiple projects, run simultaneously, so that you can test for different project patterns and evaluate differences in real time. Each team should be a unique experiment, proving or disproving something about the change program. Just be careful not to put quantity over quality.

Not all the initial projects will succeed at *their* objectives, but it's important that they be selected so that they succeed at *your* objective: proving that the change provocation adds value. All seven of our initial teams would go on to experience positive organizational outcomes from working in the new way, even though one failed to achieve its market objective. An "unsuccessful" project can still be a win for the change program if the project achieves even a negative outcome faster than normal.

And as in anything, failures can yield valuable lessons. From those first teams, we discovered what types of projects were harder to adapt to our change initiative, and which patterns yielded the quickest successes. Spotting those kinds of patterns helps you hit that 25 percent tipping point as quickly as possible.

This approach is no different from a startup with limited presales, sales, and support capacity: first you want to focus on prospects that have the highest potential for buying. Then you almost overwhelm that initial set of customers with support so that they will be successful, not worrying about scale. Scale will come later, on the back of their enthusiastic recommendations of you and your product.

The Selection Process

To select the initial seven teams, we began as you might in creating a recruitment funnel. We established three important criteria that would filter for the kinds of teams that would be properly respected as exemplars of change.

Screening Criteria One: Believers Only

When Robert LeBlanc and I first kicked around the criteria for selecting these first seven projects, we began with a shared conviction that Hallmark would work only with people who wanted to work with us. There have been endless instances of big expensive change efforts thwarted and undermined because there were too many naysayers forced to the front lines. Given that you're working with a small subset of the population anyway, better to keep those skeptics on the sidelines and let them watch (which creates its own pull, ironically).

Belief in the benefit of change is essential to change. The only way I have ever seen humans truly change is when they have a positive attitude about the change. Even when the new things may feel awkward and unfamiliar, simple self-interest in doing better work will prompt believers to keep trying to master them.

If change is offered first as an option to those existing teams that want change, then the change program is more likely to flourish and stick. So, we were interested in identifying teams led by believers at the team level (the "bottom" of the org chart) who were also within a division led by a senior vice president (SVP) believer at the top of the chart.

We decided to adopt this bottom-up, top-down lens to the selection process because we were daunted by the prospect of also engaging the many middle-level executives in between. At the time it seemed like such a huge undertaking. I mean, it took a few months just getting the dozen or so SVPs up to speed. We had no idea how to engage hundreds of middle-managers in meaningful ways, although we would learn to do that with time.

In fact, even sorting out the genuine believers among the SVPs proved to be much more difficult than finding enthusiastic team leaders. When the CEO says that "change is a good thing" you'll get unanimous agreement among her direct reports, whether they truly believe it or not. While all the IBM SVPs were nodding their heads to change, there were only some that were *bought in*. The rest had been merely *brought in*. We thought about the SVPs the same way we thought about the teams: we'd use our scarce resources only with those who really wanted in on change.

I had to trust Robert's judgment on this. While this chapter may give the impression that identifying the initial seven teams was the product of a rational sorting process, behind the scenes it was anything but. After I set out the criteria that would work best for our program, Robert's insights into his peer SVPs were essential in deciding which projects offered us the best chance for success. He knew which of the SVPs were super excited about Hallmark. He and I spent hours in his office spit-balling our assessments on which project might be too big, too complex, or, at the other end of the spectrum, too simple or insignificant. Then we'd settle on some candidate projects, and he'd recruit his SVP peers to permit those teams' designation as Hallmark teams.

I found that sometimes all a change leader can do when starting out is stick to your knitting and allow your trusted higher-ups to work their back channels for you. Our first seven teams were represented by four SVPs. It was enough variety so the senior leadership team would have multiple points of program evolution and validation, but not so many that we were constantly communicating to multiple people at the top of the tree.

With time, as I gained credibility, I got to be in on that decision-making. But in those early days, I was only vaguely aware of how much was going on behind the scenes. And that's okay, because if the company is truly ready for change, you don't need to see the so-called sausage being made. It's better to maintain your clarity of vision for those parts of the change program you control.

Screening Criteria Two: Full-Timers Only

One critical requirement for consideration as a Hallmark project was that team members had a full-time commitment to it. We didn't want key players to have their time and attention divided while working on other projects with different team practices, or who were temporarily assigned to a project for a few weeks or months.

For change to scale and stick, it must be like a door to another world that locks behind anyone who enters. The temptation to revert to old ways is strong, and people who are working on both pre-change and post-change teams rarely convert.

People who are steeped full time in change also are more likely to take their new and better ways of working with them when they do move around. As you start scaling out the number of projects, your earliest team members are still out there somewhere, helping drive change, even if they're no longer on their original project. And at some point, (in our case, it was in our year three) you have enough people in the program, and they're now being remixed onto other projects. You won't even need to touch the teams they're on, because they've become tremendous advocates for change in general and for your program in particular.

However, when a change initiative is undertaken, companies commonly like to pull some of their best people to work on a new project. But, because these people are regarded among the best and brightest people in the company, they also keep their other job (or jobs) while they're detailed to this new thing. If the new practices fail to stick, those people aren't really held accountable, because after all, their other stuff is all going fine.

In the early days of change, there will always be many more people doing things the old way, so someone with one foot in the new and one foot in the old will have a hard time overcoming the culture's old-way inertia. This makes them unlikely to become change agents—the people you need to make change go viral.

Even if part-timers are excellent people and the project itself is a success, their part-time status will undermine what you want to achieve in leading change. I hear this all the time: "We did this project, and it worked in 90 days! You can't imagine what this team accomplished. It was amazing. But now we're having trouble replicating it at scale."

"What happened to those team members?" I ask. Many times, nearly all had been loaned part-time to this special "innovation" project. Then they all went back to their other jobs working in the old ways again. Then another part-time team was assigned a similar 90-day project. They picked it up as fast as the first team. Then they went back to their day jobs. And that's how you get a two-year change project that drags along showing "success after success" while gaining zero traction and building zero ability to scale and stick.

Screening Criteria Three: Meaningful Projects Only
The only way to validate a change program's robustness is to risk failure with projects that matter. The idea of "testing change" on low-risk or

meaningless projects is a terrible one. You won't prove anything by succeeding at something that doesn't matter. No one will care, and no one will even think to copy your example. That's because everyone thinks that what they do matters a lot and is therefore far more complex than the little problem you cleverly solved. Further, small-scale success won't help the company.

For these and other reasons, Hallmark project teams had to be working on meaningful projects that were funded to deliver quantifiable business key performance indicators (KPIs). I thought a helpful bottom-line definition of *meaningful* was this: if Ginni cared about its outcome, it was meaningful. Using that definition would ensure that the SVPs were as deeply invested in the success of these projects as the core team members were. I knew we might need help from some of these senior leaders along the way, and I also knew that no one gives you the time of day if you ask for help for something they don't care about.

But how could I know which projects were truly meaningful to Ginni? I couldn't. Robert knew, and I counted on him to gauge which projects were held in highest esteem among IBM's upper management and would burnish our Hallmark program brand.

If you're looking to play it safe, you've come to the wrong place. While you'll be destined to start small, as I've discussed, it means there's an even greater responsibility to quickly prove that your change will succeed on the most challenging of projects. A big part of the job is risking getting fired. If all our projects failed, if our approach proved to be unviable, we would know it absolutely. And we would scuttle the program quickly.

Narrowing to the Final Seven: Varied Team and Project Patterns

One of the most important contributions your first teams make to the change program is that they give you the opportunity to learn how your change hypotheses react under different circumstances. Each different project type should yield insight into the versatility of your tooling and education resources, and how the program's design responds to address different needs. To do that, you need to see a variety of teamwork patterns.

For example, we wondered if our approach would work equally well for a brand-new team delivering a new product, versus a long-existing team delivering, say, software version number 20. Does it work the same for a human resources (HR) team as it does for a product team? We had to work with as many diverse patterns as possible to discover the answers.

My year one Hallmark candidate project wish list read like this:

- At least one version 1 project, a brand-new project that's just been spun up, with a new team working from a blank slate; and at least one "version 20" project, with an entrenched team accustomed to the old ways
- At least one internal-facing HR project (something that served our employees) and several projects that affected external customer experiences
- At least one project with more than 200 people on it, and at least one small project with less than 30

I also wanted Hallmark project team members to run the gamut from new-to-IBM to very senior engineers with 30 years or more with the company.

At the end of the selection, we had teams as follows:

- Team 1 had more than 400 members working on the second major release of a hardware/software product. They included people from engineering, product management, design, marketing, sales, legal, and finance.
- Team 2 had more than 20 software developers working on a new version 1 product that would replace an older product.
- Team 3 had more than 20 developers working on a new release of mainframe software that originated in the 1960s, one of IBMs oldest products.
- Teams 4 and 5 each had more than 50 team members working on existing products.
- Teams 6 and 7 had about 10 or 20 members each working on two version 1 internal projects, one that would face all employees and one that was salesforce facing. Each of these teams was sponsored by our chief human resources officer.

Of the 11 IBM divisions, only 3 made software products, but that's where 5 of our first 7 teams ended up. Product teams were ideal to start with because they work in long-lived, stable groups, characteristics that enhanced the successful adoption of new practices. Teams in our IBM Services division, by contrast, were working on very meaningful projects, but those teams were more fluid; they'd come together for work with one client and then disperse. We would need to wait until our practices matured before exposing them so directly to our clients.

One Final Catch: Agreeing to Our Rules

Because these were the first seven teams, we had frank conversations in advance about how they, in certain respects, would be functioning as lab rats for us. We needed to observe and document this new process we were trying out, and we intended to learn as much from them as they would learn from us.

To do this right, we established rules that incoming teams were briefed on and had to agree to. Some of these rules might seem intrusive (to some they felt career-threatening), so we needed the teams' explicit consent in advance. It was okay to choose not to join the program (always opt-in), but if you wanted in, you had to agree to these rules:

- Entire teams will be expected to participate in the mandatory week-long bootcamp orientation and training in Austin. The exception was the 400-member team, for which a significant number of leaders and key contributors agreed to attend.
- Hallmark program office people will be all-in on the team's business. They will attend meetings, review code and prototype artifacts, review decisions and decision-making processes. They will not work on the project, but they will often be like flies on the wall, watching and taking notes during work sessions, both to identify unforeseen obstacles and to take candid assessments of peoples' behaviors.
- As leader of the Hallmark program, I will be visiting at least quarterly with the GM of each team's business line, the SVP of that division, and with our CEO to give a presentation about your team's progress. No one on your team or in your line management will attend those conversations, nor will you be able to preview the presentations.

I faced some strong objections to this last one, all of which expressed the same general sentiment: "If you're talking about me, I need to be in the room."

I understood their concern—fear often thrives in organizations when people sense they're being discussed behind their backs. However, I assured them there were valid reasons for this rule. At IBM, as in most organizations, briefings filtered through multiple layers of management often lost their edge, stripped of any meaningful insights by the time they reached the top. I knew that driving real change required bypassing this sanitized communication process. To truly shift IBM's culture, we needed unfiltered conversations about teams' progress at the very top of the organization.

Robert worked tirelessly in the background, engaging with senior leaders, addressing concerns, and securing the necessary buy-in from the teams' leadership. Eventually, everyone accepted the rule, but it was a bitter pill for both the teams and their upline management. Fear of the unknown is inevitable during any transformation, and effective change leadership means acknowledging those fears while presenting a compelling case for the opportunities ahead.

What the initially resistant team leaders didn't realize was that their goals and ours were deeply aligned: at Hallmark, we were fully committed to their success and, indeed, wanted and needed to make them heroes. By facilitating open, unfiltered briefings at the highest levels, we aimed not just to introduce tactical practices to the top leaders but also to use them to fundamentally reshape IBM's culture. Only then would the change truly take root.

A Lifeline to Modernity

We learned a lot from those first few teams, but not always what we expected. Project patterns turned out to have almost no impact on change adoption. We assumed that new teams working on new products would have an easier time, while the more established teams would be more set in their ways and resistant to change. Instead, we were pleasantly surprised when one of the most senior teams, a legacy project for mainframe software, was able to make massive advances during their one-week bootcamp.

There were problems, *but they had nothing to do with design thinking*. Instead, there were the usual instances of interpersonal conflicts and bad manners. There were also times when upper management meddling with project scope and deadlines threatened to throw off the team's flow of new practices. The Hallmark program team managed to smooth out those problems as they arose. Finally, there were issues with IBM's obsolete software tooling, which we managed to get around in cooperation with the office of IBM's chief information officer.

In general, we found that these initial Hallmark teams began using the new way of working and collaborating more easily with hardly any direct help from us at all. When reports started trickling back that other teams had heard about their colleagues' experiences and wanted in on Hallmark, we were baffled. We didn't think we'd done that much to earn such an early vote of confidence. What we discovered was that the close attention we gave to these seven initial teams had positive benefits totally independent of the design thinking aspect.

The teams came to rely on us as their advocates for modernity in general—and they'd never had any support like that before. We were seen as the go-to people who would take up their case with HR, clear up interpersonal spats, prevent interference from above, and give them more updated tools to work with. It didn't seem like much to us, but it meant the world to them.

That's why the experiences of our first teams aroused so much excited interest in Hallmark. The teams that suddenly wanted to join weren't necessarily interested in design thinking, but they were begging to work in ways that were better than what they had. IBM teams were bursting with need for change, and we appeared to have an answer.

The lesson here is to never forget that change has a power of its own, utterly divorced from the nature of the change provocation. When you introduce a new way of working and you commit to its success, you must also promise a break from *all the dysfunctions* embedded in the status quo. For that reason, you must give your change program the authority to change everything, not just the headline practices. In the short term, you will brighten the change brand's halo effect, but in the long term you will show how change permeates the organization down to the most minute details, because that's how to achieve true cultural transformation.

Hospitality

On the Sunday before we launched the bootcamp for our very first Hallmark team, we all stayed late at the office doing final run-throughs of the next day's program.

We'd spent months architecting the bootcamp schedule, selecting the teams, planning the onboarding process, and building the curriculum. Recent weeks had been devoted to preparations that tailored the content of the program to this one team's particular needs and challenges.

Now on this late April evening, I got the sense we were all feeling motivated but tense about the next morning. As we prepared to go home, I got everyone together so I could share a few thoughts that had been on my mind all day.

"Until now," I said, "we've been in the Hallmark business. We've been in the design business. Tonight, that stops. From this day forward, we're in the hospitality business."

Some puzzled looks, a few smiles.

"Yeah," I continued. "Literally. These bootcampers are our customers. We're not doing them a favor—they're doing us a favor by showing up. I expect each of you to introduce yourself to each and every camper. Thank them for their time and be genuine about it. Ask them about their products, about what challenges they face and how they think we can help them. Genuinely let them know we are a service organization and that we are super excited that they are entering this journey with us."

If you want to make change irresistible, you must recognize how much of it resembles hospitality. Preaching the benefits of your new thing won't inspire change any sooner than a chef preaching nutrition will entice people to try the food. We don't go to a restaurant for lectures or cooking lessons. We go to a restaurant for an outstanding dining experience.

To be an effective change agent, think less like a teacher and more like a chef. Your job is to deliver an experience that is so remarkable that people will keep returning for more. Equally important, if what you deliver truly adds value, not only will they adopt it, but they'll also enthusiastically recommend it to their friends and colleagues. They will become the viral change agents on which irresistible change depends.

Takeaways

- **Team wins are not program wins:** The proof of cultural outcomes—behavioral shifts—is different from the market outcomes a team strives for. Ensure your program is tracking the right KPIs for evidence of cultural success, in addition to metrics on the better market or organizational outcomes your teams are looking for.
- **Select initial projects with care:** Choose meaningful, high-visibility projects with full-time team members who are committed to your change initiative. These projects should be diverse in size, scope, and team composition to give you multiple proof points across different organizational contexts. Prioritize teams led by believers who are eager to embrace change, and make sure they're working on significant business challenges that senior leadership genuinely cares about.
- **Culture is your business now:** By setting standards for participation, communication, and accountability, you signal that this isn't merely a process change but a fundamental cultural transformation, based on new values as well as practices. When teams join something that transcends their immediate project goals, they naturally become ambassadors for the broader cultural shift your organization needs.

5 | Driving the Adoption

When it came time to schedule the first Hallmark project team for their week-long bootcamp in Austin, I decided they should be required to show up for the first day at 8:00 a.m. on a Monday. Not only was 8:00 a.m. very early by IBM's standards, it would also force everyone to fly in on Sunday. I hated having to travel on Sundays and as the vast majority of the Hallmark team members were not from Austin, I knew this would be irritating. Then, when they showed up, they learned that their laptops were banned, which came as a shock to those who'd expected to do the usual "multitasking" to escape the drudgery of most IBM trainings. We'd previously let their management know that they would be offline except for a couple of specific times during each day.

If this doesn't sound in line with the hospitality pep talk I'd given my staff the previous night, it's because we had an important and specific objective to achieve during the first hour of the first day: from this group of 30 IBMers, we needed to flush out sources of resistance as soon as possible. While we would be excellent hosts, we chose to exert a certain amount of psychological stress at the start of the week so that anyone skeptical of the bootcamp would be more likely to make their feelings clear. They were entitled to those feelings, of course. But we needed to understand, as quickly as possible, what fears they were harboring. In these early days, learning these things were as important to us as the outcome of the team's work.

For our first exercise, we quietly distributed Post-it notes and Sharpies to the assembly of bootcampers in the main room. Faces visibly clouded over, as we'd just confirmed the artsy-fartsy aspect of all this design stuff. But then we surprised them: "Write down every reason why this week will fail. Why your team will fail. Why this transformation effort will fail."

After a brief double take, they were off! It's hard to describe the sudden burst of enthusiasm. I mean, haters gonna hate and, all of a sudden, they were writing like crazy. The energy level skyrocketed as they zipped off one Post-it note after another. Most had generated half-a-dozen or more, leaving a five-foot-by-five-foot multicolored mosaic of brutal negativity on a wall by the front door. When everyone was finished, we could see they were all itching for the opportunity to explain their objections. But we ignored all the Post-its, without comment. Instead, the Hallmark staff simply introduced themselves, by which time most campers had given up trying to hide their annoyance. Facial expressions ranged from puzzlement to mild disgust.

The Post-it wall would remain in place the whole week, ultimately bearing mute witness to how wrong everyone had been on Monday morning.

When it was my turn to talk, I stated our terms of engagement, which most team members had not yet heard directly: "For the week that you're here, you're going to play by new rules: the rules of this bootcamp, and of design thinking. You're going to be doing exercises intended to accelerate your work and make it better. But by Friday, if these new ways of working haven't driven outsized value for you and your team, you're welcome to go back to the old ways. You'll never have to see us again." That got their attention.

We could make that offer because we were confident that no team would take us up on it. And no team ever would.

Start by Building Belief

As Robert LeBlanc had said almost three years earlier: many IBMers knew change was needed, even if they didn't know or agree on exactly what that change needed to be.

Our research so far had told us that skepticism about change was two-fold. One, people doubted whether any changes could be radical enough to move the needle at a company as large as IBM. Two, there was doubt that IBM leadership would have the fortitude to see such changes through. In response to the first area of doubt, I determined we needed to shock each Hallmark team with changes so profound that team members would immediately grasp their differentiating value. To address the second, we needed to create some mechanism to demonstrate how change would work inside IBM over time.

The bootcamp was our stage-one shock treatment center, and it had these two objectives:

- Change the team's collective belief system to one that saw the value and viability of the new practices, tools, and teammates.
- Build team cohesion and rapport so that team members would have each other to lean on in the face of systemic resistance and other challenges in the months to come.

We had this team for just five days, and we had to program each of those days so that team members would become so engaged with the new thing that they would move from neutrality or skepticism into advocates. And because the bootcamp was in many ways a haven from real-world obstacles, they would also need to believe that the new practices *at least had a chance* to work when they returned to their offices. That would be a heavy lift, and it dictated that the bootcamp experience be both unusual and extraordinarily demanding.

In advance of the bootcamp, the Hallmark program delivery team had invested weeks of research into the details of the team's product, its market, its objectives, and its challenges. They had created classroom materials custom-made to guide the new Hallmark team through their next stages of software development using design thinking. By giving them new tools that would advance their real-world project's progress in just one week, we wanted to provoke a profound shift of the team's understanding of how the new ways could affect their daily lives.

At this stage, we weren't interested in perfecting the fine points of design or design thinking. With only five days to work with, our hope was simply to change their *belief* in these things. We did this by doing, not teaching. Our method each morning loosely followed a 10-30-20 pattern for each hour: 10 minutes for my people to introduce a new practice, 30 minutes of the team immediately applying the practices to their project, and then 20 minutes of group reflection on the result. Afternoons were dedicated to intense work sessions in which the team pushed the project forward, making use of the new practices they'd learned that morning. Hallmark program leaders silently hovered during those afternoon work sessions, observing and offering nudges of advice when it seemed necessary.

The opening day at the bootcamp was a long stressful day of introducing new design thinking concepts, complicated by the fact that this was a distributed team, and many members were meeting each other in person for the first time. Most of our bootcampers had little or no experience collaborating in truly interdisciplinary ways, and we knew this was going to be the hardest aspect of our work for the week. This wasn't primarily an intellectual exercise—our people were smart; they'd pick up on the tactics. What would be unnatural would be the human interaction and trust that modern collaboration requires.

At 6:00 p.m. on day one, we piled everyone into buses and took a trip to Alamo Drafthouse for a private screening of a documentary called *Design Plus Thinking*. We could have sent this video in advance as part of the preparation materials or shown it in the bootcamp, but we wanted everyone to experience it together in a theater, in a more impactful way.

We chose to screen *Design Plus Thinking* because the film concerns itself more with project outcomes than with the specifics of design thinking. The best interviews in the film involve entrepreneurs and engineers who praise design thinking for its positive impact on their careers, their businesses, and their lives. The bootcampers watching the film saw non-designers much like themselves extol the virtues of what was for them an entirely new paradigm for doing their work.

The question-and-answer (Q&A) session afterwards reflected the stress and weariness of the long day, plus some effects of Alamo Drafthouse beverages. It got real, and we were able to make the first of the emotional inroads into our Hallmark team's psyche. Researchers who study culture often depict it as an iceberg, with 90 percent of its mass below the surface in the form of such defining qualities as shared beliefs, assumptions, and values. That night, we began engaging in the subsurface aspects of their culture, and we were also learning where the most powerful of those forces might push back on us.

Every change program should try to create moments like these, when you can expose the team undergoing change to success stories from external sources they can relate to. Ideally, you want to present them with stories that show how change is useful not only to the success of the organization but also to establish trust that change can be good for them and their careers, and their personal fulfillment at work.

We were lucky to have a documentary film that suited this need. Other change programs might bring in guest speakers, find a similar documentary, or perhaps make their own short videos. Regardless of the media involved, it's important that the team member see and hear the firsthand experiences of people who overcame their initial skepticism and embraced the new thing.

The film and Q&A afterwards provided our bootcampers the chance to authentically engage on the matter, to feel their hopes for success and fears of failure, and, very important, also feel our shared vulnerability in this moment. By the end of the evening, I think the bootcampers understood that Hallmark's success (and IBM's success) was riding on their success, and that we were all in this together.

On Tuesday morning, day two, we accelerated the pace of instruction by piling on a number of new design concepts with little time allowed for questions and discussion. We were deliberately overloading the team members' heads so they would be dependent on each other to figure things out. Then we sent them back to the hotel with a homework assignment that would take them through most of their evening on their own.

On day three, Wednesday, I led a course that aimed at showing the full potential of what they'd learned over the past two days. We screened what was then a six-year-old video of Steve Jobs introducing the original iPhone. As if by magic, his words reinforced nearly every concept that we'd been pushing on since Monday morning. As Steve spoke, I could see the lights going on in the team members' eyes. The first iPhone was a triumph of design and design thinking in action. Every product launch should aspire to that standard of user-friendliness and delight.

In subsequent bootcamps over the next two years or so, this Wednesday Steve Jobs video proved to be the pivotal moment when everything clicked. All our programming, all the tension, it all resolved in that session—all the way down to the last remaining skeptic. That's when we could see that the team members had a new way of communicating and being with each other—visible evidence that their underlying beliefs had turned a corner on at least the possibility of this new thing.

The day four sessions on Thursday marked the first time we allowed the project team members to work on their own all day. We spoke only when asked for guidance, showing them how to knock down certain barriers in the work that were unfamiliar to them. Friday, day five, was reserved for their *playback*, our term for show and tell. The project team members presented their week's work to the Hallmark program team, highlighting the new insights and progress they'd gained over the course of the week. They used the new language of Hallmark and displayed new types of project artifacts based on that language. It was their first attempt at delivering in this new world. And in every case, their enthusiasm was palpable and the strides they'd made were outstanding, even outlandish.

From Belief to Adoption

Each of the first several teams to go through our bootcamp confirmed they were indeed shocked. First, and not coincidentally, the actual experience of the bootcamp and its surroundings was unlike anything they'd ever experienced at IBM. *We shocked at every touchpoint.* And, they'd experienced a significant leap in the quality of their work at an unexpected pace. But they were also aware they had made these strides in a bubble, insulated from the normal distractions of daily life. They were justifiably concerned that new things they did for five days in Austin might not survive the first five days exposure to the old IBM that awaited them. The bootcamp had made an impression, but for change to stick, the new behaviors must be adopted in the context of the organization's everyday management, processes, and systems. To move from belief to adoption requires as much attention to external hurdles as it does to the team's internal struggles.

For teams undergoing change, everyday use can be obstructed or simply crushed by any number of negative old-way influences. For example:

- Tools and systems built to accommodate old ways might hinder the new practices.
- Line management might be hostile or indifferent to the new practices and demand things be done in old formats and at the old rate of weekly progress.
- The team lacks the confidence to make important decisions based on the new frameworks.
- Teammates may revert to old practices, sometimes unintentionally.

In the irresistible change model, the change program team must take responsibility for figuring out how each of these anti-patterns are impeding a team's adoption and devise scalable solutions to each.

Within Hallmark I called this our *adoption mindset*. No matter the reason, the burden for lack of adoption was on us. Hallmark, the deliverer of change as a product, was accountable for understanding and overcoming our users' objections and the organization's patterns of resistance.

This is really no different than the kind of no-excuses mindset you might find at any scrappy startup. No one on my leadership team ever dared to complain, "Well, this group just doesn't get it." As deliverers of the new thing, we were 100 percent accountable. If a team didn't adopt our offering, then either what we were providing wasn't valuable or we were doing something wrong. Neither outcome was acceptable to us.

The adoption mindset works because it pries open a ton of creativity and innovation. Many of our best ideas arose from the difficult work of puzzling out why one or another's team's adoption was not coming around. (Another important driver of creative thinking was that accountability for adoption—not enablement—was reflected in the job evaluations and compensation of every Hallmark program team member!)

But how do you most effectively uncover these anti-patterns and come to understand all the forces that thwart adoption? As I mentioned, most of culture (and its influence) is invisible. Above the surface, it reveals itself only in the observable behaviors that are the result of what's hidden below.

That's the subtle challenge of leading and measuring shifts in culture. Altering those powerful below-the-surface forces is essential to long-term success, but evidence of those changes will always be restricted to what you can openly observe and evaluate. Are the team's operational rituals incorporating the new elements, or are they merely performative? Are they collaborating in modern, inter-disciplinary ways, or are they breaking up tasks into siloed skill sets? What artifacts are being created, and which of them are truly valued? How is management reacting to the team's progress? How are individual careers being supported as they navigate change?

Having our assessments of progress limited to these kinds of observations dictated our post-bootcamp program design. For as often as possible, we needed to be with the team members while they worked, maximizing our exposure to their ways of collaborating and their resulting plans and prototypes before we could hope to see evidence of shifts in IBM's culture—the invisible assumptions, beliefs, and values.

Our response to this formidable post-bootcamp challenge was to hire senior experts in design thinking and Agile who would work closely with the new Hallmark teams for their first few months back in the real world. These folks weren't there to directly contribute to the teams' work, they were there to *identify obstacles preventing the team from working in the new ways.* These obstacles could range from the interpersonal to the systemic. They were how we in the Hallmark program office remained intimately connected to the teams after they'd returned home from Austin. Because these expert monitors would spend most of their days quietly making observations and taking notes, internally we nicknamed them *the psychiatrists.*

Team leaders were wary of the psychiatrists at first. Who enjoys having an outsider lurking around taking notes during your meetings and reporting back on it all? Nobody—until the teams saw evidence of how helpful they could be.

For example, on several occasions, psychiatrists reported back to us about middle-manager interference that was proving to be a problem for a Hallmark team. These teams were reporting up to people who spent most of their days managing teams working in the old way, and conflict was to be expected. Sometimes the psychiatrists went directly to the middle managers to discuss these issues, and other times the problem was large enough to involve me and other Hallmark program team leaders. In a few cases, a psychiatrist alerted me to problems serious enough that I had to straighten it out at the SVP level.

After that happened once or twice, and the teams saw the clouds of management interference lifted, the team leaders recognized that their psychiatrists were truly there to help. The teams became more comfortable with sharing their concerns about other ways IBM's entrenched culture was holding them back.

Complaints from one team, for example, alerted us to certain software tool deficiencies that were obstructing the team's progress. The team was using a source code system too antiquated to support the interdisciplinary collaboration design thinking and Agile demanded. Another team leader complained that their IBM internal communications application didn't have built-in capabilities that made it easier for teams to collaborate. And there were no tools at all that supported the artifacts of empathetic engagement that are the foundation of design thinking. Because our psychiatrists were funneling all this data back to the program team, we could present a single, more compelling case for these needs to the chief information officer (CIO). Not only did we, as Hallmark, have some degree of clout, it was also easier for the CIO to respond to one group, as opposed to granting multiple, random exceptions all over the organization. When these "pilot" technologies were approved, teams looked on their Hallmark psychiatrist as a hero.

When we initiated these pilot projects with the office of the CIO, the Hallmark program office bore the initial cost of licensing and testing the new tools and accepted responsibility for their use. After a tool passed our testing, we would then pass on the seat-by-seat licensing expense to the Hallmark teams as part of their price for joining Hallmark.

As in all things about the change program, you should always look toward making yourself disappear. Eventually, as it became apparent that Hallmark was the way forward for everyone, these tools became new corporate standards, paid for and managed by the CIO. Hallmark got out of the tool business and, in fact, our CIO office spun up a team in the image of our Hallmark teams. Led by Bill Higgins, a high-ranking IBM Distinguished Engineer, the Whitewater team designed and built an internal offering that made these new tools irresistible to install, use, and maintain. Sound familiar?

In this case, it was tools. But the bigger lesson here is that your specific change provocation is only a small piece of getting the outcomes your transformation is striving for. You'll need to look at all those externalities, like tools, and figure out a strategy for improving them alongside the headline changes. It would have been useless to assert the need for something like Whitewater before we'd introduced design thinking and Agile. But once those dots were connected, they became an obvious part of the story.

Breadth Versus Depth

This description of the first Hallmark bootcamp may seem very tidy and well considered, but its rollout was far more rushed and improvisational than I've depicted it. From the day the Hallmark office opened, we were under significant pressure to quickly identify the initial teams and get them going. The program presented at the first bootcamp was the product of a contentious and tension-filled process within the Hallmark leadership team.

Charlie Hill and I got into some heated arguments about how perfect we needed to be, and when. As the chief technology officer and chief designer, Charlie believed we needed to do a more thorough job infusing the teams with design thinking and Agile practices, driving more perfect adoption of the new way of working across fewer teams. From his perspective, Charlie thought we were moving too fast, and because of his engineering background, he certainly knew much more than I did about how much education these teams would need. My concern was that we couldn't afford to spend more time and money up front perfecting a design education system. We only needed to teach them enough about design thinking methods to make an incremental *but noticeable* change in their work.

As Hallmark's leader, I saw our program more like a fragile startup that aspired to perfection but needed to survive to get there. The initial Hallmark outcomes didn't have to be perfect to gain peoples' attention. They simply had to be demonstrably better than what the teams would have otherwise achieved. If they were that—and nothing less—we were making progress and could allocate more time and money expanding our all-important footprint.

Within the irresistible change model, there is a built-in tension between the change program leader and the lead expert on the specific change provocation. Charlie was constantly informing me how excellent the teams could be, and I was constantly informing him on how good the teams needed to be. We made progress by tacking back and forth between these two competing points of view.

To gather and maintain momentum, size matters in an organization. It creates what I call the *gravity* of any initiative or competency, and it almost always equates to the head count associated with it, relative to the total head count. If you're too small to matter you won't have the gravity to attract continued attention and resources. This manifests in an organization's loss of fortitude, which spells doom for many, if not most, culture change efforts. They simply fizzle out.

In the case of the first bootcamp, we opted to create a very strong program that was hardly perfect, but good enough to help the new Hallmark teams get better very fast. The language in many of our first bootcamps was too formal and academic for my taste, but that was all we had to work with at that point. Even the charts and graphs we showed had been borrowed from university design courses.

As we moved from one bootcamp to the next, the program kept evolving dramatically, and I think the tactical outcomes also improved. By the time we were onboarding our seventh team, the experience had shifted substantially to something that was distinctively an IBM program, with terminology of its own, and with outcomes that would rival anyone's best.

The necessity of learning from our first seven teams had resulted in a much better product for the benefit of team number eight and all the teams beyond. We now had a program that had been so thoroughly workshopped and polished that it could be distributed to other instructors. Charlie had complete confidence we could teach it and hand it off, which is perhaps something we would not have been so assured of if we'd started out taking months to develop the perfect program.

It turned out that taking longer to provide a better program at the start would have been a waste of precious time and resources. For one thing, you don't know what you don't know. I'm much more inclined to launch a prototype in the real world, and adjust quickly to the feedback, as opposed to trying to perfect version 1.

The moral of the story is that you should get your program started and not worry too much if you feel underprepared. The path of change will teach you lessons you never could have learned any other way.

Empathy, First with Ourselves …

I received one such lesson several months in, while visiting one of our teams. They weren't struggling with the usual obstacles to change—instead, they were fighting about empathy itself.

Empathy for the end user's experience stands at the heart of design thinking. Our new ways of working emphasized understanding and addressing user needs above all else. For this particular team, it seemed they'd taken this principle almost too much to heart. The designers, engineers, and product managers had each developed their own interpretations of the user research, leading to competing visions of how to best serve their users' needs. What began as passionate advocacy for users had devolved into territorial disputes, with team members locked in heated arguments over who truly understood their users better.

"We've won the battle but lost the war," I remember thinking, "now everyone loves their users but they hate each other!" The irony wasn't lost on me—in their fierce commitment to user-centered design, they'd forgotten to extend that same understanding to each other.

The solution emerged in what seemed at first like an overly simple mantra: "Empathy, first with ourselves, then with our users." When we proposed this as a new shared cultural value, the teams embraced it immediately. This simple reordering of priorities transformed their dynamics, making collaboration and compromise natural extensions of their work rather than obstacles to overcome.

This insight proved valuable beyond just internal team dynamics. We observed that many team members, particularly designers, would often bristle at what seemed like arbitrary demands from upper management. While we wanted IBM's leadership to embrace design thinking principles, we also needed to acknowledge that some organizational constraints simply can't be negotiated. In any place of work—private sector, public sector, or nonprofit— market pressures and other external demands will dictate timetables and deliverables, regardless of whether a project team believes its work is "finished."

The solution was to extend our empathy principle further: just as team members needed empathy for each other, they needed empathy for their broader operating environment. The Hallmark office developed intensive exercises to help designers understand their unit's business strategy and tactical challenges. We even created an innovative way to make business fundamentals more engaging: a quarterly video conference that broadcast live IBM's earnings calls. Inspired by the cult TV show "Mystery Science Theater 3000," we assembled a panel of business-savvy designers alongside experts from our chief financial officer's office and other business divisions to provide real-time interpretation of the earnings call for our global audience. This unique format made the language of business accessible and even entertaining for everyone.

This deeper understanding of IBM's business transformed how designers approached their work. Instead of resisting tight deadlines or resource constraints, they began developing creative compromises and interim solutions. More important, they gained insight into the pressures facing their business-focused teammates and managers. Over time, many designers discovered that this broader empathy became their "superpower"—enabling them to gain influence and equal standing with their business partners. They learned that the path to having a seat at the table wasn't just through design excellence, but through understanding and engaging with the full spectrum of business challenges.

Managing Demand

Thanks to our successes with the first seven teams in our year one, we could use a new metric for Hallmark's rate of progress in year two: the high level of demand for Hallmark slots. We knew we were on our way when we had a backlog of IBM teams willing to pay for that privilege. We trusted the organization—like any marketplace—to place value on things that were working.

It wasn't very long after our first few teams had launched that the Hallmark program office started getting unsolicited expressions of interest from other SVPs and other GMs. On a few occasions, one of the SVPs would come to me and say with some urgency, "I've got this project that's really important. I want it in Hallmark." Much sooner than

I had anticipated, we had aroused demand from sponsors of important projects that everyone at IBM would recognize as impactful—the exact kind of projects we wanted.

The demand grew so fast that it became unmanageable. I had to ask our systems head Pierre-Henri Clouin (PH) to also start serving as our business development manager. With so many incoming requests for our limited time and resources, we needed PH's knowledge of IBM and its people to catalog all the application requests and advise us on our selection criteria.

PH put together a marketing deck about the program so that he didn't have to keep recounting how Hallmark works and what to expect as a participant, as a team leader, and as an SVP. He went on the road and gave presentations with the marketing deck to attract new applicants and build what was from our perspective a marketing funnel. Then, for his sales pipeline, each applicant team leader was interviewed and provided information about their project so that we could perform due diligence and rank them based on an updated set of criteria:

- Which SVP is affected? We never stopped looking to grow our footprint. Projects under SVPs with few or no prior Hallmark teams were a priority.
- What is the work pattern? New project? Existing project? Second version? Twentieth version? We kept an eye out for work patterns we knew produced quick wins while also looking for patterns and business units that were new to Hallmark.
- How big is the team? How many locations? On how many continents? We always wanted to expand our global reach.
- Based on the team's work deliverable commitments, when would it make sense for them to onboard? Sequencing the project into our schedule was often the deciding factor between two similarly attractive projects.

All these factors figured into deciding which IBM projects became Hallmark teams in year two and beyond. On a rolling basis, we maintained a backlog of about two years, making give-and-take adjustments along the way. Sometimes a team would jump the line based on changing conditions, not the least of which were IBM's shifting priorities. With far more demand than we could ever serve, we were in the enviable position of choosing only the best and most impactful teams that wanted to work with us.

We tried to sort out which teams to take next partly based on whether the team's product cycles coincided with open slots in our bootcamp schedules. It wasn't always possible to make such a match, and there were times when a Hallmark team came out of the bootcamp full of enthusiasm, only to be forced back into working on a project already halfway out the door. For example, having been awakened to the value of user research while in Austin, these team members were now expected to complete delivery of a software product with no user research at all.

We rarely ran into such troubles in our first bootcamp teams, because the bootcamps had been sequenced to send the teams home at the start of a new product cycle, and they could apply all their new practices to this new software version. But when we started adding more teams in year two, the sheer volume prevented us from sequencing things perfectly. One team might arrive in April and return to work using old approaches to push out a June release. We ran into that a lot, and I'd have to get involved because all those team members had just gotten a week of costly training, and now they were getting forced to unlearn it all. We'd work team by team on various workarounds.

This kind of conflict became constant as the number of Hallmark teams approached triple digits. When we began jamming dozens of teams through our bootcamps, there was no way to optimize any of their team start dates. We came to accept that the transition to the new way of working would be different for every team and that some transitions would be more disruptive than others. All we could do was communicate our concerns, add support, and do our best. Yes, they will have forgotten some of the stuff, and it would cost us to do a little extra coaching and supervision. But we trusted they'd get on track eventually. And they did.

Above all, we had to keep the momentum of change going. Inevitably that meant for some teams, change didn't necessarily begin right away. Change began for them with a shrug, "Okay, we're going to release what we already started, but we'll get it right next time." Progress over perfection.

A Clear Path to Scale

By the fall of Hallmark's year one, demand for more teams so far outstripped our capacity that our funding for year two was secure. We onboarded another 25 project teams in year two, closing in on a milestone of 5,000 IBMers who'd adopted our new work patterns. At that point, Hallmark had a momentum of its own, limited only by our ability to manage our rate of growth.

That year had also marked a particularly sweet moment of validation: we returned to that same annual Technical Leadership Summit where Charlie and I had been all but tarred and feathered not so long ago. But this time the program format was different. Thanks to Hallmark's success, the summit had been reimagined into an interdisciplinary product workshop, with simultaneous custom bootcamps run by my team and other experts from across the business. We onboarded dozens of new Hallmark teams in just one week. By the end of year three we'd touched another 200 teams.

Long before that, we knew we were well on our way toward achieving culture change for all of IBM's 400,000 employees. We could barely respond to the demands of the immense number of teams in our backlog. That number, which climbed beyond 400 before we stopped counting, remained our single most reliable metric of success. It told us that we had succeeded in making change irresistible.

Takeaways

- **First comes belief, then comes adoption:** Design shocking, immersive experiences that dramatically shift teams' belief systems about what's possible, followed by intimate, ongoing support to ensure adoption sticks. Initial belief is essential but insufficient; without structured support during the critical transition period, teams will revert to old ways when faced with organizational resistance.
- **Own every adoption failure:** Take complete accountability when teams fail to adopt new practices, treating each instance as a design flaw in your change program rather than resistance from teams. This *adoption mindset* forces your program team to continuously innovate solutions to organizational barriers and creates a no-excuses culture that drives creative problem-solving.
- **Balancing breadth and perfection:** Focus on expanding your program's organizational footprint by helping more teams achieve *meaningful improvement* rather than pushing fewer teams to *perfect implementation*. A noticeable upgrade in outcomes across many teams creates greater momentum than flawless results from just a few, especially in a program's early stages when building credibility and demand.

6

Communicating
the Progress

All our program work up to this point was still only half the story. None of that work would have made an impact on the larger organization if no one knew about it. The other half of the story involves the attention and resources we invested in our communication strategies.

Even after two years heading the business process management (BPM) unit, I still didn't know much about how communications functioned inside an organization the size of IBM. Whenever our unit had new products to announce, we'd work with the communications people assigned to our division, and they would take care to make sure the marketing message was getting out to our customers and partners in the space.

Now as head of Hallmark, where the product was change, I wasn't sure what corporate communications could do for us, apart from announcing our existence in an internal news release. I knew we had three strategic challenges. The first challenge, at IBM's senior leadership level, was over-coming skepticism that such change could be scaled. The second challenge, at the team level, was to overcome skepticism that these specific changes produced better outcomes and made peoples' lives better. And the third was demonstrating to the broader IBM population that change was continuing, that the company was displaying the fortitude to see this one through.

How could IBM's communications people help us tackle these three challenges? Initially, it didn't occur to me that these even were communications related.

I knew enough about corporate interpersonal communications to invest plenty of time keeping senior leadership informed. That's why I insisted on those quarterly briefings on Hallmark teams with the corresponding general managers (GMs), senior vice presidents (SVPs), and often with Ginni herself. A 15-minute call every 90 days, if it was frank and thorough, would be enough to keep them apprised of progress and earn their continued confidence and support. But that was only part of it.

The whole truth included using those meetings to enlist their help reinforcing positive behaviors we saw on their teams. While there was fear on the part of the team leaders that I'd be complaining about them, in reality I did the opposite: in those GM/SVP/CEO meetings, I specifically highlighted individuals who were enthusiastically responding to the changes, and I even drafted emails of thanks to each of these individuals and requested that the senior leaders send them under their name.

Try to imagine what happens when a Hallmark team member in Chicago, Singapore, Dublin, or Prague sees in their inbox a personal communication from their GM or SVP saying, "Hey, quick note. I had an update from Phil today. Thank you so much for doing the good work!"

Heads exploded. Not only were the individuals proud, and their behaviors reinforced, word got around fast that the C-suite had their eyes on Hallmark teams, that this change program is real and it's how you can make your mark at IBM.

Good message, right? But how to get it out at scale? I was about to learn.

The *X* Factor

Usually at IBM, a program office of Hallmark's size would never have its own communications director, but we were lucky that Robert LeBlanc anticipated our need. He asked Melissa Sader, his division's top communications person, to share some of her time with us in that role. Melissa sat on my leadership team, attended all the meetings, and became the "protein spike" that connected our program to the broader, existing communications team. It turned out that Melissa's knowledge of IBM and its corporate communications culture was absolutely essential to our effectiveness. She knew how to speak in IBM language across the organization, and she knew what people would accept and what would turn them off.

Certain innocuous-sounding words have unfortunate connotations in any culture. Changing the culture requires that you figure out which parts of the language are accidentally reinforcing old behaviors, or, alternatively, where you can change certain words to signal difference. For instance, someone would refer to a Hallmark workspace as a design *lab*, and Melissa and I would always correct them. It's a design *studio*, we'd explain. Studios were designed from the ground up to foster greater collaboration and drive the "intentional serendipity" we coveted. Of course, the word *lab* can mean all that, too. It was simply a signal. The word *lab* at IBM was in use already, and labs had become fairly routine office environments, like the siloed offices and half-lit hallways of our old Austin facility. At IBM, the word *studio* was new, and we could define what it meant as a piece of the new world. It was emblematic of the culture we wanted to become.

Melissa also knew what communication resources we could draw on and how to use those resources to maximize our impact. At Melissa's suggestion, we shot video at the end of each bootcamp capturing the campers' fresh enthusiasm for the new way of work. Melissa saw to it that the following week a three- to four-minute edit of these interviews was prominently featured on IBM's intranet.

These post-bootcamp interview videos turned out to be highly effective in reducing skepticism about change—one of our key communication objectives. They also addressed our other objective: assuring the entire organization that change was continuing to happen, that it wasn't a one-and-done thing.

The videos ultimately set the tone for all our communications going forward: there would be no traditional evangelism. The team members from Hallmark projects—not the design program leadership—would do the talking. The stories of mainstream IBMers, in their own words, would be how we would communicate our successes. We mostly promoted comments from non-designers who would tell their story of real-world change happening at IBM, and what it meant to them. It was so much more impactful than having me or one of my team talk about our vision of the changes we foresee, or offer hearsay evidence.

Skeptics will always have an easy time belittling the idea of change as a pipe dream or a fantasy. But when a veteran lead engineer goes on camera to claim that Hallmark has changed their life for the better, there's not much left for the skeptics to say. It's difficult to hate on the firsthand story of a trusted peer.

We communicated in planned and deliberate ways to the audiences that were most important to Hallmark's success, putting emphasis on real-world changes and successes. These communications efforts delivered against all three distinct strategic directions: up, down, and globally:

- Communicating up was mainly my responsibility, through the one-on-one report outs from me to senior executives covering the work of the active teams in their area.
- Communicating down was the job of the Hallmark program team members assigned to do outreach to candidate teams and to onboard new participants for the week-long bootcamps. These communications were both bespoke based on a team's specific needs, and also at scale, using the bootcamp videos to help prepare them for the changes they'd be experiencing.
- Global communication was what we called the internal communications run by Melissa, which included preparing those highlight reels of the bootcamp attendees and securing their prominent position on the intranet home page and in senior leadership communications.

With time, I started calling communications our x factor because it served as a force multiplier for all our other program functions. Thanks to Melissa's access to IBM's main corporate communications center, she was able to talk up the exciting and innovative aspects of our program with her peers and identify people in other divisions who were open to change and could help us.

It only became apparent to me after Melissa was added to the team, but my deep reliance on communications made sense because the irresistible change model is based on running a change program as though it were a small startup. With 400,000 IBMers as our target user base, we enjoyed unlimited access to a captive and relatively homogenous market. We just needed a strong communication capability to make the most of it. The mode for reaching that market was through our three essential communication strategies, which proved to be as critical to Hallmark's success as the role of marketing and public relations would be for any startup.

Strategy, however, frequently involves choosing things *not* to do, and there were a lot of activities we didn't pursue that are standard communications fare for typical change programs. Each time a new team was added to Hallmark, we did nothing to hype the team's new status. Typically, only the team members themselves and their management chain even knew they were in Hallmark. And while my appointment as general manager of design had been announced in a company-wide communication, I tried not to make too much of it. The news caused a stir among IBM design thinking acolytes all over the world, and soon enough invitations arrived requesting I meet with them to promote the program. I politely declined almost all these invitations, because even though I love talking about design thinking and its impact, that kind of communication strategy would not have moved the ball a single inch toward any of our objectives.

I'll admit, this choice was also a communications tactic for burnishing the Hallmark brand appeal. Getting in on Hallmark's exciting change program was a strictly pay-to-play proposition. Limiting these messages to a select few was a strategic carrot that, ironically, accelerated our broad adoption

In general, especially in the early days before we had hard evidence, I didn't spend time standing up in front of audiences promoting how design thinking organizations are *x* percent more productive with *y* percent improved stock performance. Early on, I had some brief discussions like that with senior leadership, but beyond those dozen or so people I never wanted to evangelize what *could happen*. Our discipline was only to report what change *had happened, through the testimonials of those who had experienced it.*

Most corporate change programs assume they must evangelize to create a sense of urgency for change and recruit people into the change movement. But actions speak much louder than words. Is that news to anyone? In the irresistible change model, the communications focus should always stay on the operational change that is occurring in the real world, versus delivering an evangelical vision of what change could happen. This has the practical benefit of keeping your messaging very focused. When you stick to the plain authentic facts about what is happening now, it's much easier to develop clear, intentional approaches to your communications channels, messaging and sequencing.

If you think about it for a moment, the wisdom of sticking to authentic first-person testimonials is backed by a decades-long shift in that direction for all customer relationships in our culture. Madison Avenue visions of the future aren't nearly as powerful these days as personal endorsements from social media influencers. In the software industry, where software is now sold mostly as a service, you no longer see lavish demo videos tempting you to buy before you try.

Change programs need to meet their market where it's at. It's likely that the user base for your change program no longer buys anything based on big promises about the future, and they're certainly not apt to jeopardize their careers on that kind of vision. It's safe to assume they're not that interested in hearing about the change you claim will happen. They'd much prefer that you make the new thing available and help them use it and evaluate it for themselves. Then maybe they'll adopt change. All communications in a change program should support this path to adoption if you want to make change irresistible and take it to scale.

The Audiences for Change Communications

Without a broad rally-the-troops change movement message for everyone's ears, your change messaging requires a more nuanced understanding of who each key stakeholder is, what's important to them, and how best to reach them.

- Senior executives at the top of the company (in our case, the CEO, her directs, and their directs) need to see signs that the change is being adopted successfully and can spread and scale throughout the company. The message: change is scaling.
- The team members of the teams undergoing change and their upline management (line executives) need to be nurtured before, during, and after their kickoff experience, in our case the bootcamp. The message: change is working, and it can work for you.
- The entire company not yet involved in the change needs to see concrete evidence that change is taking place, that people engaged with change love it, and that it's already meaningfully affecting the company. The message: change is spreading.

A quick example of how this targeting played out. Starting from day one of the first bootcamp, top leadership was intensely interested to learn how change was going over with the first seven teams. We encouraged them to talk with the Hallmark project team members in their divisions to get their firsthand accounts. Of course, showing how the teams were adopting the new ways and loving them was the main focus of year one.

As glowing as the reviews were, I never stopped worrying about what that small number communicated to the senior leadership. So I tipped my hand when I could to show that we were laying groundwork to accommodate more than triple the number of teams in year two and then triple that number again in year three. I constantly spoke about the present in the context of a rolling three-year plan. Additionally, when I reported on the year two hallmark growth, I noted how much more efficiently they were being onboarded, reducing per-user costs.

This is a good example of shaping the message to fit the audience. Reducing Hallmark per-user costs was of little interest to everyone but senior leadership, for which it was a serious concern. Our year one Hallmark project team members were having a great time learning this new way of work, but if their example couldn't be replicated economically a thousand times over, then we were all wasting our time and the company's money. In year two, our ability to efficiently scale was a major concern of the senior leadership—and no one else.

It's easy to skip over this sensitivity to audience messaging if your program communicates with more generic evangelizing messages. In my experience, to make the most of your access to internal communication channels, it's worth your time to really understand the different people and audiences you need to influence in order to be successful. Each group has a different stake in change, and you put change in danger if you don't communicate with these distinct audience needs in mind.

Communicating Up with Candor

I spent a significant amount of my time preparing for the quarterly one-on-one meetings with senior management, which frequently involved repeated rescheduling. Even in year one, every 90 days I had one-on-ones with at least nine of them—four or five GMs, four SVPs, and Ginni.

A typical rule of thumb is eight hours of preparation for each really great one-hour meeting. If you consider these were 30-minute calls, and it's probably four hours of preparation for each, that's a full week out of every 13-week quarter that I'm spending on these meetings. I'm not in the boot-camp classes, I'm not doing design or any of the fun stuff. It's yet another case in which the most important work of change looks nothing like change, and what you think is work is not the work at all.

These meetings were critical for a number of reasons. Communicating status of their teams, for sure, but also the optics that communicated to everyone in their organization who would see time being spent on the change program. Calendar time is the single most precious resource of any-one in a large organization, so the fact that we were given that access was another of those signals.

I soon discovered that even when the CEO says "Meet with this guy every quarter" it doesn't always happen! Of course, I understood that in those early days of Hallmark there were many things more important than our fledgling change program. But even as some meetings kept getting knocked back, I couldn't let them slip entirely off their calendars for the entire quarter.

On one of those occasions, I called Robert to say, "I'm having a little trouble getting on so-and-so's calendar. What do you think?"

He let me in on the secret of getting on people's calendars, which is getting to know the people who control those calendars. At IBM at the time, it was the administrative assistants and executive admins who con-trolled access to each executive's calendar, and if you didn't have some rap-port with these gatekeepers, you were unlikely to get on the schedule ahead of someone they did know. This was another fact of life inside IBM that I wished I'd understood sooner!

Fortunately for me, my own administrative assistant, Denise Reierson, was a well-regarded long-time member of IBM's administrative assistant community. She cultivated a network with her peers in areas with Hallmark teams and, suddenly, I was getting meetings scheduled, and they stuck.

On my part, I never canceled, never changed any of my scheduled quar-terly meetings with senior leadership, always deferring to their schedules. I had to look at their reality with empathy. On any given day, they might have three critical fires to stamp out, and maybe Ginni's calling once a day about each of them. I was accommodating when I knew that someone was facing real crises, but I also never let a quarter go by without that 15 minute one-on-one update.

The GMs were in many ways the most important to Hallmark growth because they were closer to the teams where the work gets done. I really hated to get put off by a GM with two or more Hallmark teams reporting to them. I put special emphasis on getting the GMs' active participation however I could, especially among those who found it easy to blow off Hallmark as a small program that wasn't yet affecting them at scale.

We bond with people when we do meaningful things with them, and that's the quality of experience, however brief, that I sought with the GM. Prompting them to send those emails of praise to model members of Hallmark teams was one way I could give GMs an activity that connected them to Hallmark and demonstrate their support for what the teams were going through. And, of course, every GM understood that I also had a one-on-one scheduled with the SVP they reported up to, a mild form of pressure that provided its own encouragement.

One last thing. In the beginning, it was important that all of these meetings were truly one-on-one. First, it allowed for a level of candor that change requires. We didn't have time to beat around the bush, or else the outcomes from the program would be delayed and the program put in jeopardy. But just as important, this created a social dynamic that simply doesn't occur if everyone's in the same room. Teams knowing that they would be candidly discussed without their input was a check on them. Same with the GMs. And the SVPs knew they were getting unfiltered information from me, so when I asked them to commend someone, they were happy to do it, reinforcing everything from a positive perspective. It was both negative and positive reinforcement that accelerated our success.

Communicating Everywhere with Authenticity

In contrast to the relatively opaque nature of evangelizing, all of our communication strategies emphasized transparency in their tactical execution. But there's a fine line between evangelizing and telling the positive stories of team success. Staying inside of that line was critical to me because I knew that eyes would just start rolling, especially among the tens of thousands of people change hadn't yet touched.

When leading change, the clarity that comes from communicating tactics with complete transparency is absolutely essential to success. Transparency keeps it simple and invites fast fixes. It's what makes transparency worth the effort. If you're communicating with transparency and things don't look good: fix the things. Transparency also has a way of generating frequent unintended and unexpected beneficial outcomes.

The simple, transparent reporting system we used to communicate the progress of the first few Hallmark teams was so useful that it evolved within four years into a full-blown management architecture tracking hundreds of IBM teams with tens of thousands of employees. Our reporting structure was so faithful to recording what had happened that for IBM GMs it became a reliable tool for tracking progress and projecting future outcomes for all their teams, not just their Hallmark teams.

Think about that the next time you develop a slide deck. Is it faithful enough to the reality of your operations that it could be used as an effective management tool? Or does it lean more toward the promotional evocativeness of evangelism, with more factoids than facts, with cherry-picked data instead of the most important and enduring key performance indicators?

What this meant for most of year one is that almost all meaningful communication was dependent on the reviews we were getting at the team level. Were the teams changing? Were team members adopting the new way of work and liking it? That's all everyone wanted to know, from the top senior management to the next wave of new teams considering applying for Hallmark status: was this new thing any good? And, of course, the global community of IBMers wanted to know: are we keeping at it?

Melissa's bootcamp video spark of inspiration was key to figuring out that authentic, tactical voice that we wanted to adopt. As the final day of our very first bootcamp drew closer, all of us could see the program had made a difference for the project team members. We could read the excitement on people's faces and hear the delight in their voices. But only Melissa saw that excitement as an opportunity to create a valuable communications asset.

Halfway through the week, Melissa said to me, "These people are loving it. We need to get them on video." She wanted us to capture their enthusiasm in interviews before they all headed back home on Friday.

I thought it was a great idea, and two of the program team folks seized on it right away. One was an amateur photographer who sped out to the nearest photography shop in Austin and returned with two digital video cameras, a green screen backdrop, lighting, and other equipment. Their instinct was, "We're going to make this cool. This is not going to be just putting a quote in PowerPoint."

That was Wednesday afternoon. When I arrived on Thursday morning, the duo had already turned one of our small storage rooms into a photography studio! The walls were covered by all the colorful Post-it notes dripping with the negativity that bootcampers had filled out on day one. The look and feel of the room communicated that it was fresh and new, not at all a typical IBM environment.

The next morning, we had one final session that ended about 11:00 a.m. and we told everybody, "Before you leave for the airport, we want to get you on video. We've got three questions for you, and it will take you 60 seconds, a minute and a half at most."

And then our newly formed video team ran in to get them seated, lighted, and mic'd up while Melissa asked each of them the same three questions:

- What do you think about your week here?
- What had you been you expecting before you arrived?
- How do you plan to carry this momentum back to your teams?

For a few of the most enthusiastic interviewees, Melissa added a fourth question: "What happened that flipped a switch in your head?" She wanted to capture that aha! moment for everyone to see.

The best comments in the videos came from veteran engineers with years of IBM street cred, self-admitted skeptics who looked into the camera and confirmed they now believed in this new way of working. A good example is the top-ranking IBM Distinguished Engineer who marveled how the new way of working could have saved his project 100 person years of work on their most recent release.

Other glowing reviews included the following:

"This was the best week I've ever had at IBM."

"We made more advances in one week than we'd made in the last three months."

Over that weekend, I sat down with my laptop's iMovie app and went through more than an hour of the video we'd captured. I listened to all the quotes over and over again (which were music to my ears) and when I came up with a story narrative, I started moving the clips around to support the narrative. I edited it down until it was between three and four minutes long—a "greatest hits" sizzle reel of IBMers acting more excited about their work than they had been in many years, perhaps ever.

Melissa got us a slot front and center on the IBM intranet that first week, and for the next eight or nine months that became our space, more or less. Every time we concluded a bootcamp, I'd personally edit the video over that weekend.

Once the video was ready and posted, Melissa made sure the corresponding SVPs and GMs communications teams were aware that employees in their division would be highlighted. I wanted them to know that Hallmark was contributing to their unit's "fame."

As for distribution, I felt it was very important to make the video available online by Monday or Tuesday of the following week. It's not just that I wanted the material to be current and fresh. I was also mindful of the spirit-dampening effects that returning home might have on some of these team members.

How can I put this? One function of the video was to tie these team members to their positivity, to get them to own their ongoing enthusiasm with their own teammates. We couldn't risk having them begin doubting the value of design thinking because they'd been sucked back into the dominant culture at their IBM workplace. With the videos being posted online, we made them *heroes* for all their colleagues to see. After that, it was in their self-interest to keep being heroic.

I mean, if the people at work think you're a super hero because they saw the video, you're not going to tell them otherwise, are you?

Of such dreams change is made.

Every Detail Matters

Back in 1964 when the eminent communications theorist Marshall McLuhan wrote how "the medium is the message," he was the first to show how the impact of communications is often less about their content and more about their mode of transmission. Consider how the impact of communication varies among, say, texting, video calls, and in-person conversations. Each medium has its own dynamics, constraints, and social norms that mold our patterns of interaction and thought. I'm simplifying, of course, but suffice it to say that in times of change, your chosen message medium sends signals as powerful as the content of your message.

The Hallmark program was about change, so I wanted every message we sent out to be about change, but also the form of the signal itself needed to communicate change. In simple terms, we made sure that everything we produced out of the Hallmark office—bootcamp materials, pitch decks, video testimonials—was a thousand percent higher quality, more engaging, and easier to use than any other IBM materials. We were unanimous in the importance of Hallmark standing out in this way, and we obsessed over every detail before sending any Hallmark artifact out into the organization.

For example, for those quarterly calls, the Hallmark team dashboard and deck we provided to each SVP and GM was designed to communicate the highlights better than any other IBM dashboards and reports they used every day to manage their work. It started with our choice of format. Back in 2013, IBM standard dictated use of the older PowerPoint screen format based on older computer screens with a boxy aspect ratio of 4:3, typically called standard definition (SD). Every PowerPoint at IBM was formatted that way, and many of the projectors at IBM could only accommodate that SD format, even as the modern world had long moved onto the cinema-style 16:9 aspect ratio and high definition (HD) format.

I told my team that everything Hallmark put out would be in the newer HD format, even if most projectors at IBM could only handle our decks at reduced size.

I also dictated that we would abandon IBM's standard PowerPoint format and share documents and decks only in PDF format. I preferred PDFs because they could be locked, so no one could mess with our data and our distinctive look. I'd seen people at IBM futzing with PowerPoints, changing the fonts to smush words together and even altering content to eliminate inconvenient information. This was anathema to our focus on tactics and transparency, and PDFs offered a simple solution.

These may seem like small things. And they *are* small things, but that's the point I'm trying to make. Every aspect of communicating change needs to be part of an integral whole creating the emotional impact of *moving forward* into a better world. We never said this explicitly, but at every touchpoint we wanted a jarringly different reaction from the norm, result-ing in a "Wow, this *is* different. This is *better*. I *want* this!"

Within about a year, sort of organically, all IBM presentations switched to HD format, and offices with the old projectors had swapped them out. Our commitment to high-quality communications—the medium and the message—made it happen.

This is a lot of work, with a lot of painstaking attention to detail. Today would we move from PDFs to vertical video? To a podcast style audio update? Perhaps. The only thing for sure is that it would be different from the status quo. It would feel like movement and look like change.

New York Times Calling

At some point every change program needs a certain degree of external valida-tion to give all our internal stakeholders the fortitude to stick with it. Early on, as we were showing our first signs of progress, I was pushing Melissa, "Hey, get us in the business press." I didn't want to evangelize; I just wanted to tell the media the stories about what Hallmark teams were achieving. We were on a bold path, had done some good things, and deserved recognition. And if IBM people read that in the business press, that would help us. It would fortify the internal perception that Hallmark was good for IBM.

Just a few years earlier, I had experienced firsthand how fast a few out-side voices can provoke a rapid shift IBM's internal groupthink. While I was head of the BPM unit, we set out to radically simplify our product portfolio. Salespeople hated the idea, warning us that discontinuing certain products risked losing some loyal long-term customers angered by having recently purchased a product that would now be obsolete.

I tried to explain why we shouldn't worry, that if we are transparent about our reasons and provision them into the new streamlined product line, our customers would understand. These words for the most part fell on deaf ears among the salespeople, who braced themselves for the backlash as we reduced the BPM unit product line from 44 to 4. The positive customer feedback started rolling in soon after. Customers liked fewer products. They told our salespeople they appreciated how we were simplifying their lives. And then, like throwing a light switch, all these worried salespeople fell in love with our new slimmed down product line.

All it took was a few good reviews from customers to make the sales-people do a complete 180 degree shift in their attitude toward our product changes. I felt excited by the idea that a little bit of positive media attention could create some buzz about IBM's new human-centered design direction and those voices might create an echo chamber loud enough to ensure senior leadership maintain support for Hallmark as we scaled up.

But when I pestered Melissa to get Hallmark into the business press, she assured me it was way too early for IBM's big public relations (PR) machine to work with us. Meaningful business results weren't there yet and we could end up in an emperor's new clothes situation—bragging about things that lack meaningful substance. I had to agree that she was right but I never stopped pushing on that door, hoping one day it would open.

Soon enough, though, word was getting out. There were two external constituencies that started pinging Hallmark with interview requests: the business press and tech industry analysts. Melissa and I both had concerns about how ready we were to handle the inevitable "gotcha" questions from those quarters. Lucky for us, IBM PR is a very carefully managed machine, and they had no intention of exposing me or my team to press interviews until we had gotten professional media training.

We flew into Manhattan for the day-long training, and it's something I'd recommend to anyone who seriously wants to grow as a communicator. I went in considering myself to be a fine natural communicator, and the first thing I learned was how little I knew. An interview is an opportunity to tell your story of change, and not about directly answering the questions they ask. The teams that communicate best have developed a common message and practice the skill of taking questions that are off the point and bringing the conversation back to the common message.

Everything was recorded in our practice sessions, and then we had to watch our tapes and get feedback from our group. For some teams this part might have been awkward, but the Hallmark crew was pretty tight. We were all open to the training and were comfortable being watched by the group as we each stumbled through the exercises.

It was really eye-opening how much we'd learned in a single day, and although as I recall the training was crazy expensive, it was well worth it. I found it was helpful even in my internal communications within IBM. There is a professional discipline in forming a message and staying on message. It seems reasonable to get some good coaching in that discipline if you believe, as I do, that communication is a critical lever in scaling a change program.

I would soon put all this to use when Ginni Rometty's letter to investors in the IBM 2015 annual report marked the first time Ginni went public with our transformation:

> IBM Bluemix, our platform-as-a-service for developers, was created by IBMers using Agile and Design Thinking approaches. It has grown rapidly, ending the year onboarding 15,000 developers a week.

I was overjoyed when I saw this because I knew we'd hit a real milestone. The CEO's annual letter is like a corporate version of the State of the Union address. Everyone at or near the top of the organization scrutinizes every word and having Ginni publicly embrace design thinking and Agile gave us license to push even harder within IBM.

It also gave Melissa more than enough to work with in pitching IBM's public relations team to consider Hallmark as the subject of a mainstream business press story, perhaps in the *New York Times*. The PR team is accustomed to doing publicity that supports product releases or announces award winners, and Hallmark didn't fit either template. The PR team's first thought was "Well, nobody's going to care about that." But there was one highly influential team member who saw some promise in the story, and after a number of conversations with Melissa, she agreed to try to "place" the story idea with one of her journalist contacts.

They were very excited that Steven Lohr, a veteran *New York Times* business reporter who had written about IBM for many years, indicated his interest. Arrangements were rapidly made for me to fly to New York and sit for my first big media interview.

But I said, "No, that's not the way to do it." I wanted Steve to come to Austin and experience our changes firsthand, in our new spaces, with our people authentically working in our new ways.

And our PR person said, "I don't know if he'll do that."

I repeated to her that this was the only way to do it, here in Austin. I hated the idea of sitting there in Manhattan and going blah, blah, blah about design for an hour or more. It would be evangelism, it would be a selling thing, and I've got nothing to sell. To write knowledgeably about the changes that were happening inside IBM, I was convinced Steve had to come to Austin and experience it for himself.

Steve agreed to come out, but it took a few months to work it into his schedule. When he arrived, my whole team and many Hallmark people met with him in our studio. He witnessed firsthand the energy, the intention with which we designed our new environments and the dramatic changes we were inserting into our tooling and processes. We talked to him as we would any other guest visiting our studio.

That was about March 2015, and I have follow-up emails from Steve dated mid-June, so he was still working on the story then. Sometime about August, he told us the article had been submitted to the Sunday business section, but there was no telling when it would run. We waited months before our PR person wrote me saying that the story would run Sunday, 15 November 2015.

I saw it online first, then picked up my copy. Under the headline "IBM's Design-Centered Strategy to Set Free the Squares" the entire top half of the first page of the Sunday *Times* Business section. There was a cartoon image of a person with a bright blue cube for a head, and a butterfly popping out of its top like a jack-in-the-box.

The story began:

> *Phil Gilbert is a tall man with a shaved head and wire-rimmed glasses. He typically wears cowboy boots and blue jeans to work—hardly unusual these days, except he's an executive at IBM, a company that still has a button-down suit-and-tie reputation.*

Over its 3,000 words, the article described the Bob Dylan photograph in my office, told how design thinking works, quoted an academic impressed by IBM's hiring of 1,000 designers, and reviewed the company's recent triumphs and troubles. Finally, Steve got around to quoting Ginni Rometty:

> *Ms. Rometty is pulling other levers to accelerate the pace of change at IBM, but she said, "Design thinking is at the center."*

At the article's end, Steve also gave Ginni the final words about IBM's 104 years of change: "[D]on't underestimate us. This is in our DNA, this ability to transform." In between there were some great lines from the lead technologist at one of our clients, for whom a Hallmark team had integrated sales data with hand-held mobile devices for store associates. He told Steve, "They've completely turned us around…we're working with the fast company part of IBM."

I've always felt like the linchpin quote in that article was one of our senior vice presidents (SVPs), John E. Kelly, who was not one of the original four SVPs who were totally bought-in with the change. He was more brought-in than bought-in, so his observation carried special weight. He was a convert to design thinking, and now he's telling the *New York Times*, "In the past, we changed what we were working on, but we were pretty much working the same way," he said. "Now, we're changing *how* we work too. And the how element is always related to speed."

Exactly the words I wanted in the echo chamber.

Communicating a Brand's New Values

The Hallmark program began in 2013 and within five years it had so thoroughly changed the IBM work culture that the practice of interdisciplinary teaming had shifted from novel to normal. Since about 2018, all work at IBM, both internal as well as with clients, has relied on co-creation as naturally as it relies on texting, Post-its, and coffee.

The creativity and passion for human-centered excellence could be found in every hallway, on every campus and in every division. Change was no longer an aspiration; it had substance and style. And now, with the *New York Times* and others documenting things, a bit of cachet.

In February 2022, IBM announced the launch of its most significant new brand campaign in more than a decade, meant to accelerate innovation with its clients and partners around the world.

The name of the new platform: "Let's create."

That wasn't marketing mumbo jumbo. "Let's create" was the honest transparent expression of what IBM had become. Nothing more, but certainly nothing less.

Takeaways

- **Testimony, not evangelism:** Focus communications on authentic firsthand accounts from team members rather than visionary proclamations from program leaders. Team members' genuine enthusiasm carries more credibility than any management messaging, especially when they describe real improvements to their work and careers.

- **Messaging targeted to each key stakeholder group:** Executives need evidence that change is scaling broadly, team members need reassurance about how change benefits their careers, and the broader organization needs proof that change is real and spreading. Each audience has unique concerns that require tailored communication strategies and distinct metrics of success that matter specifically to them.

- **External validation can strengthen internal resolve:** Strategic external communications at key milestones can drive outside-in feedback that provides reinforcement to keep leadership committed during sometimes lengthy or difficult transition periods. For example, a thoughtfully placed *New York Times* article or CEO mention in an annual report creates an echo chamber effect, reflecting back into the organization as validation that skeptics can't easily dismiss.

7

Finding the Magic

By the time the Hallmark program reached year three, a natural bell curve of performance emerged among the 50-odd teams we'd engaged. There were stellar teams at one end and decided laggards at the other end. The worst-performing 10 percent teams had such obvious flaws that we usually knew the necessary remedies. Many of them, for example, were struggling because they simply needed more time and experience due to their highly technical domains. Other teams, we found, were producing poor results because they'd been denied adequate access to end users. In those cases, we had to go to their management and explain that product teams can't reliably improve the product if they can't study the work habits and preferences of their users.

There was one poor-performing team, however, that was in a class of its own. The team leaders were all on board for change, but one highly influential engineer on the team was hell-bent on disrupting the new practices. The team was a traditional engineering-heavy IBM group, which gave the engineers an even stronger position to assert their will.

We knew this team might be a hard nut to crack, and we assigned our most senior program experts to work closely with them to smooth things over and keep them engaged. But after several weeks of this special attention, the team was still getting nowhere. The negative influence of this one senior engineer was obstructing all progress.

Pierre-Henri Clouin (PH) came to me and recommended the team be removed from the Hallmark program. We'd never done that before, but our rules had been clear from the start: you had to want to succeed. If your team didn't try the new practices in good faith, we could remove your team from the program and focus our attention elsewhere.

I approved PH's recommendation, and he sent a simple email to the team's leader that explained that we were removing the team from the Hallmark program, pulling our resources because it was clear our assistance wasn't wanted, and therefore adding no value. We knew we were testing the boundaries of Hallmark's influence, and we wondered what would happen next.

We got our answer in less than an hour. Robert LeBlanc called to tell me the senior vice president (SVP) of the fired team's division was livid. After I updated Robert on the details behind our decision, he understood and asked that I call his peer and sort it out with him directly.

This particular executive was among the two or three SVPs who I could never be sure had truly bought into the changes we were introducing. He only had a few teams in the program, in perhaps the most technically challenging of all the IBM product divisions. In my quarterly visits with him I couldn't gauge his sincere level of interest. I was able to reach him immediately on the phone, and he listened intently as I described the dysfunction we'd observed on the fired team.

"Give me a week," he said. "I'll take care of it." He asked that in the meantime we keep working with the team, and I agreed.

The episode left me grinning from ear to ear. We'd kicked out a team for rejecting change, and within an hour the news had hit the top of the organization, where our decision earned a firm vote of confidence from an unexpected supporter. In that specific moment I knew we'd won. Our culture change virus was unstoppable.

Within days, the problem engineer had been reassigned off the team. Change happened quickly after that, and within months this team went on to become one of our standout successes.

The Middle Eighty

The top 10 percent of our teams were our natural athletes, and we didn't have to worry about them. The bottom 10 percent took hand-holding

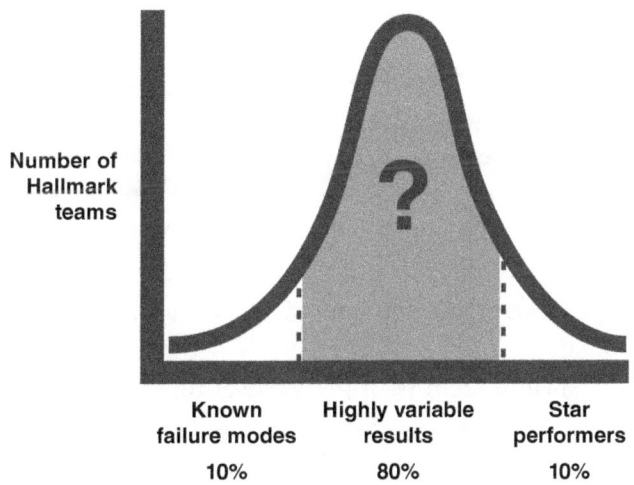

Figure 7.1 Quality of Hallmark team outcomes.

and needed time, but they weren't really a part of my daily concern. The scale the program needed to achieve could only happen if we upped the game for the middle 80 percent, so that's where I turned my attention (see Figure 7.1). And they posed a baffling problem. While all the middle 80 seemed to be trying, some teams were achieving excellent outcomes while other teams seemed to be churning. Why?

We had no answers. Outwardly, the churning teams looked the same as their better-performing peers. From both our psychiatrists' reports and from my own observations, they all seemed to be behaving the same way, generating the same kinds of artifacts on similar schedules.

And yet, despite their best efforts, the subpar teams were falling short in both the timeliness and the quality of their outcomes. Many were delivering better results than they had while working the old way, but it was clear to me and my team that their work output was lackluster and didn't fully benefit from the new practices. These teams seemed stuck, generating artifacts but churning endlessly, failing to make the decisions necessary to move the product out the door. We kept increasing the quality of our support in terms of tools and experienced designers but results across the middle 80 remained uneven.

What Is Unique About Success?

In the irresistible change model, we had to assume the fault was ours. These teams were our customers, and we needed to find out how we were letting them down. Fortunately, as a design program, we had some very good people with expertise in ethnographic research who were keen to explore mysteries of this kind. I asked Jordan Shade and Hal Wuertz on the Hallmark program staff to study our teams in depth and try to answer the question, "What's unique about the teams achieving success in the middle 80 versus those that aren't?"

Jordan and Hal brought fresh perspectives to the task. They were both early in their careers, having been hired right out of university, and had fresh takes on every problem they'd tackled. They shared a healthy sense of humor about organizational BS. I knew I could rely on them to not be shaken off by any sacred cows, either of IBM or from our own Hallmark program. For almost a year, Jordan and Hal reviewed the results of all the Hallmark teams and interviewed the team members. Their final presentation concluded with amazing and unexpected insights about the critical factors that separated the best Hallmark teams from all the others.

The most important finding was that every top-performing team had at least one team member whom Jordan and Hal couldn't easily classify, so they called them *magic people*. These were ordinary team members (not team leaders) who often stepped up beyond their day job and exercised ad hoc leadership within the group during times of uncertainty and doubt. When a team became blocked or divided on a critical decision, the magic person was the one member who put in extra effort, often during off-work hours, to gain a consensus for moving forward. These people came in all kinds of personality types, but what they shared was a high level of commitment to the new practices, and high levels of respect from their teammates. That's why they seemed magical.

Studying Magic

As soon as we heard the magic people concept defined, everyone in the program office recognized real-life examples of such people on Hallmark teams. What I found so fascinating was that each magic person I could think of had their own brand of magic. The extroverts among them would do things like convene ad hoc workshops to wrangle out some sticking point, or they might jump in and say, "Let's whiteboard this thing." The introverted magic people, on the other hand, succeeded just as well by other means, by holding their teams accountable behind the scenes, going quietly to one person, hearing them out, and then going to another person with the opposite view and finding common ground.

Only about half the magic people were trained designers, but all of them had thoroughly internalized the team's objectives and had the gumption and sheer fortitude to bring coalitions together. They had a collaborative mindset and seemed to know how to win over hearts and minds under pressure. They did what I'd call the *connective tissue work* of bringing the team back on course, restoring the focus to the new work practices before they had a chance to fall back into the old IBM ways. They also had "street cred." They knew how IBM worked, and they knew how to work its systems. That was part of the reason people on both sides of any argument held the magic people in high regard.

Sports teams have long relied on a certain type of player who sustains the team's culture of winning in the face of adverse events like injuries and losing streaks. In his great book, *The Captain Class: A New Theory of Leadership* (Random House, 2017), author Sam Walker writes how baseball managers often refer to those players devoted to team cohesion as *glue guys*. These are well-respected players who make sure that over the course of a long season the team doesn't fracture into cliques or become distracted by outsized egos. Their most valuable contribution may not be points scored or allowed but in holding their teammates accountable on and off the field. Walker cites the work of the late Harvard social psychologist Richard Hackman in singling out four common qualities found among excellent team leaders of this sort: emotional maturity, personal courage, a vision of how things ought to be, and an understanding of how to get the team to that place. Missing from Hackman's list are such traits as talent, skill, and charisma. "To Hackman," Walker writes, "the chief trait of superior leaders wasn't what they were like but what they did on a daily basis."

The teams lacking such a glue person often functioned like a shadow version of higher-performing teams. They would do the visible steps of design thinking or Agile almost in a performative way without ever using the practices to drive the business goals of the team. This was difficult to figure out at first because all new teams adopted a kind of fake-it-till-you-make-it approach as they ramped their maturity. But the teams who exercised the practices performatively did not really change and neither did their results. Improving outcome quality depends on authenticity in the execution. It was the magic people who took it on themselves to drive that below-the-surface change.

It was also immediately obvious to us that the magic people were among IBM's most important carriers of the change virus. In the previous year, we'd occasionally catch wind of a team that was successfully using our design thinking practices and had even hired designers, all without our knowledge. When we looked into it, we discovered that the driving force for change on such teams was typically an enthusiastic non-designer who had trained at a Hallmark Bootcamp. After they had completed work with their Hallmark team, they moved on to a new team, where they sold their teammates on adopting the new practices.

Jordan and Hal organized working sessions with some of the magic people to help us determine exactly how their special traits manifested, and what kind of support they needed. We couldn't keep calling them magic people, so we rebranded them as *Coaches* and put a full-time Coach community leader in place to start corralling magic people all around the company.

It's crucial to understand that *Coach* was a formal role, but not a dedicated role in our model—it was an additional responsibility people chose to take on. Also, we discovered that coaching, in our context, wasn't a teachable competency. You can nurture it, and you can give the role institutional support, but you can't manufacture a Coach through training alone, just as you can't arbitrarily train an athlete to be the one voted to be team captain. You can say it's an application of leading from behind, most of the time. It's an avocation, not a job.

We developed a detailed heuristic framework that identified the types of actions and outcomes that would point to likely Coach suspects, then through a suite of digital touchpoints, we provided resources to nurture those individuals and the broader Coach community. But we were constantly wary of efforts to dilute the brand, even as the company wanted "more Coaches, more quickly." It went back to our adoption mindset. Coaches weren't the result of "enablement," they were the result of "adoption."

One of the first things our community leader did was to get all of the folks we'd identified together online in a Slack channel so they could trade strategies and perhaps find other Coaches to help take some work off their hands. Thanks to this Slack channel, the Coach network became far more useful and in more ways than we ever could have imagined. It was the first of many such guilds across the organization. The global Coach community became a valuable forum for scaling change, because once there were hundreds of Hallmark teams, there was no way our tiny office could address all their questions. But people could always go to the Coaches' Slack channel and find some answers.

That same community also became a tool for new team formation. Oftentimes we'd be asked about the best team makeup for a Hallmark project and so now, in addition to staffing a team with people who'd had previous design thinking and Agile experience, we tried to ensure that important new teams also contained one or two first-rate Coaches on board. That's another reason for making it a priority to identify magic people. You want them gaining experience and then once they start performing well, you can intentionally move them to other teams in the organization to accelerate spread of the change virus.

Sometimes we had to ask a team to share or give up one of their magic people because we had a new team forming with a difficult mission and an urgent need for high-quality coaching. Occasionally, horse trading would be the result. "Okay," I'd hear at the other end of the line, "but what are you going to give me if I give you my 'Scottie Pippen'?" As the change program went to scale, the Coaches became regarded as extremely valuable players.

Being a Coach signaled a broader commitment to IBM, that you were thinking every day about more than the narrow concerns of your own role, even beyond your current team. We leveraged the Coach community whenever we were hosting clients in the Austin design studio. They were a great resource for exposing the program to outsiders because they could be counted on to speak with knowledge, energy, and enthusiasm about the changes that Hallmark had on their team.

Also, when some executive in, say, Singapore would pop up and say, "Hey, could you facilitate a workshop for our client at the local studio?" we reached into the community to find a Coach in Singapore, and ask if they could take half a day to go work with this group. This was an immense force multiplier for our global communications effort. Instead of flying a Hallmark staff member to the other side of the globe, which we often did in the pre-Coach days, we could count on our magic people there to step in.

Thawing the Frozen Middle

One remarkable and completely unexpected finding from Jordan and Hal's work was their discovery that all the best teams had an unusually supportive middle manager. More to the point, these were executives who actively protected their teams from interference from above. They had the confidence—and the guts—to take on higher-ups, shielding their teams from counterproductive meddling.

I suppose Jordan and Hall could have called these people *guardian angels*. Instead, they opted to call out these executives' most vital function: *shit umbrellas*.

Reading this, you may have the same immediate reaction I did: of course! It was obvious once it was said. The phenomena of shit raining down wasn't unique to IBM; it's inherent in all hierarchies. It's just part of a large organization's noise. But these disconnects between old way hierarchies and new way agility wreak havoc on change. That shit becomes more than just noise. It stops change dead in its tracks.

Enter the shit umbrellas. These were executives who, despite having no new tooling, stood up for their teams. For example, there was a Hallmark team assigned to develop the next firmware updater for IBM computer chips used in large data centers. Our designers on this team were told from the start that the immediate priority from high up in IBM was to deliver a "one-click update" function in the next firmware release. Who wouldn't want the ease of a one-click updater?

But when the team's designers visited several data centers and talked to the people tasked with updating those chips, they discovered *none* of the users needed it. In fact, a typical comment went something like this, "The last thing I need is a one-click updater. Your existing process is fine, I don't need that to be faster. What I need is to know what's in the update, and if I can trust it. I need to know if you've had other clients install it, and their experiences. I need to understand whether it's going to be a rolling update or whether it requires a reboot."

If the team had followed the directive from above, they would have wasted hundreds of hours building a software feature that no one would ever use. And yet, it almost happened—except for the highly respected Distinguished Engineer leading the project. He believed the researchers, so he stepped up, way above his pay grade, and served as the team's shit umbrella. He managed to deflect the mandate from his higher-ups and got that feature shelved in favor of delivering on the identified needs of the users. Months later I met a client at a conference who told me that this latest firmware update was "the best release in 20 years." An irresistible firmware update, who knew?

This is just one simple example of how shit umbrellas support their teams by enabling them to do their work properly. For middle managers, this issue goes far deeper. Middle management is perhaps the toughest role in the organization; it's where top-line strategy connects with real-world operations. Upline reporting tools and accountability interface with the artifacts and project progress coming from the teams down below.

Change—any change—breaks this interface just as surely as the new ways of work down at the team level broke their old tools. Like that client who said they were now working with the "fast side of IBM," our thousands of executives were being asked to manage two types of teams, with very different operational characteristics. And while we'd explained the changes their teams would be going through, *we'd done nothing to help them manage those teams.*

The revelation that came from Jordan and Hal's work was this: middle managers weren't resisting change, they were simply unable to translate it to their world. Those that figured this out on their own were our shit umbrellas.

All this left me humbled. I had focused almost all our attention and time on the teams at the "bottom" and the SVPs at the "top." In my head I had dismissed middle management as "the frozen middle," which I now realize was a costly mistake. That pejorative term (popular among some change management experts, including myself) was unfair. I thought back to my years of complaints about middle management and had to conclude, "Oh, no, it's not them. It's me. I'm the problem."

We needed to course-correct, and fast. I asked Doug Powell, who led our Hallmark Education & Activation group, for his team to step in. With the information Hal and Jordan had gleaned, it didn't take his team more than 30 days to put together a very lightweight four-hour course. It explained the executive mindset we were seeking to achieve, the kinds of artifacts they should expect to see from their teams, and what value these artifacts created in the context of building a product. It gave them a framework for how to reconcile those artifacts with existing upline expectations. The course also instructed the managers on how to probe their teams to assess the behaviors, artifacts, and decisions that manifested on the best Hallmark teams.

From then on, we had a new Hallmark rule: each new team's upline management all the way up to Ginni Rometty had to commit to having the training within 90 days of the team entering our program. This should have been the rule from day one, because our plan all along was that this new way of work was destined to become IBM's *only* way of work. Therefore, all our execs needed the tooling to know how to manage in the new world and translate their teams' operations into the existing corporate management system. And that tooling is different from the change provocation itself; it's not the new thing, it's about *how to manage teams that are using the new thing.*

We ran the very first of these courses with Robert LeBlanc's leadership team, which sent a strong signal about its importance.

For whatever change provocation you pursue, you will give yourself needless headaches if you neglect to give middle management the tools to manage both the new and old teams at once. I regret we didn't recognize this sooner. Middle management is not your enemy. What middle management needs from day one is the tooling and the training to manage the teams engaged in your new practices.

From Insight to Scale

We were on the move toward almost 100 Hallmark teams with more than 5,000 IBMers having adopted our new work patterns (see Figure 7.2). This was a remarkable achievement because, at the time, we didn't know of any other institution that had minted that many people using design

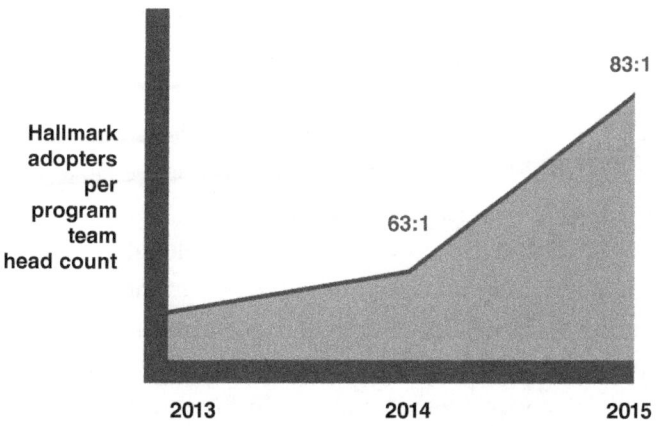

Figure 7.2 Beginning to scale: tracking the number of Hallmark head count per program office head count.

thinking in their everyday work. Doug told me he already had his Education & Activation team thinking about the next 5,000 and how quickly we could get them.

But now with the newfound insights into the scalability of outcomes, using magic people and shit umbrellas around the world, I had different plans. At one Friday leadership team meeting, I congratulated Doug for reaching the 5,000 IBMers' milestone, and then I said it was time to press our advantage. I wanted to leverage all our momentum in a major way.

"I know our entire approach has been based on intimate touchpoints, and it's been successful." I said, "But we're no longer the only experts. Others can help us. There's a maturity outside this room that's not being leveraged. We need to expand to 50,000 users in the next 12 months."

They looked at me like I'd lost my mind. The nervous laughter around the table said it all: "Is Phil serious?"

I was. I didn't know exactly how we'd do it, but I knew the conditions inside and outside IBM were right. Our goal of converting 25 percent of our market—100,000 IBMers—was starting to look less like a dream and more like an attainable target. It was time to strike, and I had complete faith in my team's ability to figure out the changes needed to hit this goal. The next 50,000 IBMers in our program could draw support directly from experienced peers—our first 5,000 change pioneers.

The economics and logistics of hitting this target forced us to consider online digital platforms for sharing our practices, tools, and target behaviors. We could now begin offering online training and certificates or badges to denote each person's skill level in the new thing. But, we were 100 percent aligned on the idea that it could never turn into the enablement approach to change. Adoption was still our mindset.

Because of all that hands-on work, we'd developed a deep understanding of how team dynamics played out in the best of them. It was always best to have a healthy mix of expertise, with a fair share of veterans and novices, and, of course, now we'd add a magic person or two and would ensure there was a shit umbrella somewhere up above. In the early days, we could handpick team members and assign designers to fit the bill. Those days were gone. Having badges issued to people that reflected their skills would give us a way to measure and scale team mixes more easily.

With the newfound understanding of the four key roles that accelerated team success—novice, expert, magic person and shit umbrella—combined with excellent online tooling and qualitative assessments, we hit our seemingly impossible one-year goal of 50,000 IBMers working in the new way. We'd set the pattern for exponential growth in year three and by the end of year five, a quarter million IBMers had design thinking experience and badged credentials—far surpassing my most optimistic projections.

While startups look to achieve an ever-higher ratio of revenues/head count, what we counted on was an escalated ratio of badges/head count (see Figure 7.3). In our third year, we began to see the kind of "hockey-stick" inflection point in number of badges issued I was looking for, and we did it without increasing head count inside the Hallmark program office.

We started with the Practitioner badge, our gateway drug. You could earn a Practitioner badge online by watching several instructional videos and taking a few brief quizzes. The function of the Practitioner badge was to identify people who were familiar with the principles and the vocabulary of design thinking. It was intentionally a low bar. This became a prerequisite for joining a Hallmark team, which meant even novice teammates were conversant in the language from day one.

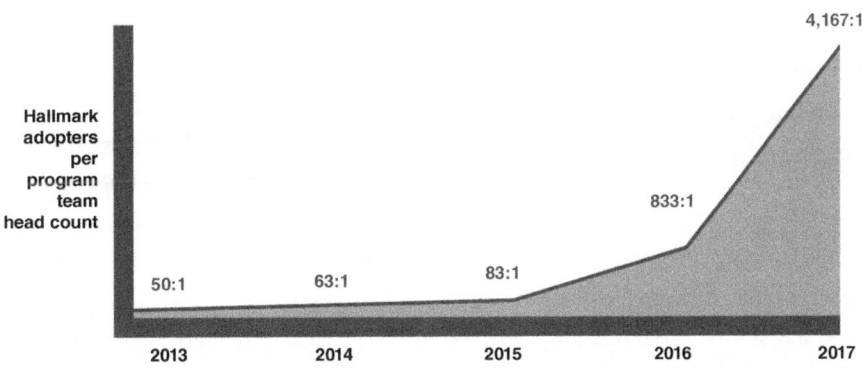

Figure 7.3 **The combination of online resources coupled with expertise that had been embedded in the business helped us achieve tremendous economies of scale.**

We raised the bar with our Co-creator badge. The user completed the online course but would also submit evidence of being on an interdisciplinary team and delivering something to market. *Market* could mean different things—maybe it was an external product, or maybe it was something internal like a new human resources tool. One team, for example, tackled how to improve the experience of becoming a first-time manager at IBM.

Doug's Education & Activation team built a community of expert design thinkers who evaluated thousands of Co-creator submissions from across IBM. These weren't just looking at final products—they scrutinized the journey maps, empathy maps, and stakeholder maps that showed how people got there. Sure, it meant more back-end work for us, but it ensured that the badge stood for something. Co-creators were people who had truly adopted these new methods.

These badges became powerful ways to quantify team health. When forming new teams, having a mix of badge levels indicated maturity—some folks would be unbadged (like new employees), many others would have their Practitioner badge, and the fewer Co-creators would be there for higher-level expertise.

We awarded Advocate badges—Jordan suggested we hand out shit umbrellas but was overruled—to all the executives who had gone through our new training. That gave us access to assessing the health of various business units, in terms of how many executives had Advocate badges. While it was hardly a perfect system, we found that having even one or two badged Advocates in a team's chain of command made a real difference in performance.

The crown jewel of our badging system became the Coach badges reserved for our magic people. To earn a Coach badge, a person had to submit real-world coaching accomplishments, work they had performed and the outcomes they generated that would help attest to their suitability as Coaches. We had three or four Hallmark program team members dedicated just to identifying candidates for these badges because, at first, people didn't really understand what the badge meant. We had to be intentional, visiting teams and finding those special individuals who naturally took on coaching roles. These were reviewed in detail by a peer group of already certified Coaches, and then it was the sole qualitative decision of my Coach community leader whether someone got their badge. We kept our standards high because Coaches are scarce; they're the Knights of the Roundtable, the keepers of the flame of cultural change.

Changing the Changers

Coaches and Advocates proved to be critical missing pieces in our original architecture of change. They became major factors in accelerating IBM's culture change because they each addressed the challenges of inside-out change in a way that worked together to reinforce each other. As middle management became more comfortable and knowledgeable about Hallmark's rituals and artifacts, having more teams working in the new way became more attractive to them. And as more and more people became badged as Coaches, they could be more intentionally deployed to spread design thinking throughout the organization, finding receptive middle management Advocates already in place. A perfect flywheel effect had been discovered, and then intentionally driven into the program.

Yet, their discovery was far from preordained. Because the Hallmark program was designed like a startup, where future "sales" were dependent on the references of our prior "customers," the real-world performance of every team was critical. Understanding why some teams succeeded and other teams failed wasn't simply good corporate citizenship—it was existential to the Hallmark program itself. And like any startup, we knew we had to embody change ourselves as we discovered emergent traits of the organization or, as in the case of Advocates, our own blindered biases. I'm not sure that a typical change enablement program (funded to teach everyone the new thing) would have sufficient incentives to learn and change within itself this way.

If you're committed to change, your change program must remain open to change itself, because otherwise it's easy to miss important things right under your nose. For three years we tried to bring a mindset of empathy to IBM's culture, and then we discovered our own blind spot: our lack of empathy for middle management. And in the wake of our successes, we also took too long to implement digital training to capitalize on the presence of changed conditions in our marketplace.

I wish I'd understood the importance of developing Coaches and training Advocates before Hallmark was ever conceived and, certainly, today I would put these in place day one. They turned out to be two of our most powerful levers along the path to change. (As an aside, if I had to do it again, I'd find a better word than *coach*, something similar to our Hallmark naming choice that didn't have preconceived characteristics. The word *coach* has become so overused that it now carries some unneeded baggage.)

When your change mission is focused on culture, rather than some new tool or method, you're more likely to discover critical insights you never would have imagined. In the end, so much about what we learned from the magic people and shit umbrellas had almost nothing to do with design and everything to do with organizational behavior and culture. One of the most important principles of culture change is that the what you are working on is not nearly as important as how you are working. That's the essence of the genome/virus design of the irresistible change model. It's also why this approach to change is an enduring one because the what of tomorrow is unknown.

Takeaways

- **Identify and cultivate magic people:** The magic people— formalized at IBM as Coaches—serve as *glue guys*, binding team- mates together and preventing them from reverting to old habits during moments of uncertainty. By creating a dedicated Coach community with rigorous standards, IBM built a network of change agents who could be strategically deployed to accelerate adoption across new teams. Coaches are one of the most important factors in scaling transformation.
- **Middle management can be your ally:** Equip middle manag- ers with tools to translate between new team practices and exist- ing systems, transforming potential blockers into *advocates* who protect and accelerate change. During the change period, they will be managing at two speeds, with teams operating in old ways and new ways, which presents a unique challenge among change's stakeholders.
- **Make adopters visible:** Create a certification system that quan- tifies adoption across multiple key personas, enabling strategic team formation, and creating a flywheel effect that accelerates the spread of change throughout the organization. Even in early high-touch days, use tools like digital badges to identify people who have adopted the new approach so you can more easily track program footprint and the growing skill sets throughout the organization.

8

Raising the Money

All change programs must start out demonstrating their worth by pushing change. Then as momentum gathers, the organization will start pulling for change. At that point, the change program must shift gears, stop pushing, and start collaborating with the forces pulling change forward.

We started out pushing change in year one by giving it away for free to the first seven Hallmark teams. It took only six months, in the middle of year one, for IBM teams to start lining up asking to join Hallmark. With the fall planning cycle about to rev up for year two, we had to adjust our approach from push to pull. With the second wave of teams pulling for change, it was time to determine how to start charging for admission to the Hallmark program.

I sat down with Robert LeBlanc to prepare for the coming fall plan and to chart our course for the years ahead. By design, the trajectory of our change project depended on our ability to attract paying customers. As I've said many times, and cannot overstate, if teams and their sponsors won't pay you to help them change, they won't adopt change. Not really. Now, as senior leaders grew impatient for more change, Robert and I had to puzzle over a few questions. We had barely gotten three teams through the boot-camp process, but the usefulness of Hallmark's new ways of working was becoming apparent, and teams seemed to be loving them. What Robert and I couldn't know was how much they loved it. Is it a little better, a nice-to-have thing? Or was it a lot better, worth allocating scarce budget dollars?

If they were willing to pay the costs of serving them, it would be the ultimate proof our program of change was, in fact, irresistible.

As one-week in-person events for 30 or 40 team members, the bootcamps were costly to produce and often required more than $100,000 in travel expenses alone. Hallmark had covered all these costs for the seven teams in year one as a part of our push for change. But for year two, when we anticipated accepting 25 Hallmark teams, Hallmark couldn't possibly cover those expenses. Assuming these teams were truly pulling for change, asking them to pay for their bootcamps seemed like a reasonable request.

At the same time, Hallmark in year two would continue to cover the considerable costs of hiring and paying the designers assigned to these 25 new teams. The way Robert and I saw it, keeping the program's designers on our payroll would give us the control required to match the types of designers to the team's needs and to ensure there were enough designers to make an impact. Robert worried that if we asked the teams to pay for everything in year two, they would also expect all the rights of management. For example, they might want to move those designers around on a whim or even fire them. "If they buy it, they can break it," Robert observed. We agreed it would be best to save that stage for year three, giving us another year to increase the organization's maturity in the management and use of designers.

To my startup mind, this entire phased-in approach was consistent with the way an early-stage company keeps tuning its business model to accommodate its market needs and access to capital. I thought of Hallmark's year one funding as a pre-seed round type of thing. We were pre-revenue, didn't have a product, and no certain product-market fit. That round of funding, if you will, was the fuel to help us deliver version 1 of the product and determine if we had early validation of product-market fit. That is, forgetting price for a moment, would people actually use our product? The answer was clearly yes. Hallmark teams were outperforming their past and their peers, and demand from other teams was on the rise. Then for year two we'd move to a one-time purchase, if you will, versus the subscription model that absorbing new head count would entail. In the startup analogy, it meant getting to revenue but also continuing a net burn as we grew. In year three, we'd move to the full subscription model, moving the designers onto their teams' head counts, and all new external hiring would be done by each team or business unit.

In terms of strategy, this felt like familiar ground. My personal focus shifted away from team dynamics (which I delegated to other Hallmark leaders) and toward the financial necessities typical of startup dynamics. The business model we'd chosen required Hallmark to start functioning like any other IBM vendor, with the defined objective of raising millions from IBM senior leadership to fund rapid change.

Creating the Sales Pitch

Up to this point, our one-on-one meetings with senior leadership had consisted of reporting on Hallmark team successes and setbacks, with virtually no discussions of budgets and future planning. Hallmark in year one was a pretty small program, not costing the leaders anything in a direct financial sense, so simply communicating what was happening was enough to keep them engaged.

That approach was well short of what would be required to motivate them to buy our product. The task of managing 25 year two teams within the IBM budgeting system demanded of us some completely new skills and tactics. As our buyers, senior executives needed reliable budget projections that forecast strong growth in Hallmark teams within their purview.

To do this effectively, we needed to train all our attention on this small but important set of stakeholders. These were the senior vice presidents (SVPs) and general managers (GMs) we'd already begun building relationships with, but now we needed a much better handle on them and their world. Hallmark would have to compete effectively for dollars that were already being pulled a half-dozen different ways. We'd done okay so far, but we needed to raise our game significantly, because as time went on, the stakes would only get higher, as would the pressure on us to deliver at scale.

I asked Doug Powell to help us figure out how to take on this challenge. Doug was an experienced senior designer whom I had brought into the program office because he, like Pierre-Henri Clouin (PH), had a strong sense of how to communicate the outcomes and benefits of design thinking to IBM leadership.

True to his background, he advised that in the same way we'd done with our Hallmark project team members, "we have to approach each SVP/GM as our user and understand them in a deep and human way." He compiled a list of traits his research showed were common among our senior executives, with specific advice on how to address each one:

- **Super busy!:** Keep the meeting to a tight 30 minutes, or less.
- **Data driven:** Frame the discussion on quantifiable data.
- **Opinionated:** Anticipate a strong viewpoint and add provocations that draw a response.
- **Competitive:** Being in the top quartile of any stack rank against their peers was a motivator.
- **No bullshit:** Wanted data, not evangelism. Remove frivolous extras from deck. Six slides total.
- **They will believe!:** They were advocates for change, but skeptics of most change programs. If they trusted us and we brought proof, they would invest.

Regardless of your specific organization—commercial, military, nonprofit, whatever—I don't think you'll go far wrong if you take into account these six common traits among senior leaders.

With these critical points in mind, we decided to begin by reconceiving the nature of our quarterly meetings with each of these critical people. This was an important starting point because calendar time with those folks was at a premium, and we had to design a more structured format for future conversations, one that would drive the funding conversation forward. PH designed a disarmingly simple new presentation deck that for the first time asserted common, objective success metrics applied to the Hallmark projects under each executive's purview.

We aimed for 15-minute meetings, so PH kept the deck very short—four slides that in hindsight should have been only three:

1. Slide one restated and reinforced the overall mission of Hallmark. It took 30 seconds, but it was something I felt was important to state at

the top of every meeting. Repetition is good, and also the fact that the mission was *always* the same reinforced the discipline and longevity of the program.

2. Slide two was meant to stoke the GM's competitive instincts. It listed how Hallmark was doing throughout the company. It was just a one- or two-word bullet for each of the macro program elements we wanted to highlight status of: number of teams, upcoming bootcamps, designer recruiting status. We even included real estate updates, new tools introduced, and other details that gave the manager a sense of how they were doing compared to everyone else.

3. Slide three recounted the ways in which design drives better outcomes. The slide seemed necessary at the time, a palate cleanser between the second and fourth slides, but if I had it to do over, I would delete this slide and include some of its points in slide one.

4. Slide four was the money slide. Tailored to each manager's specific realm, it listed the status of all the manager's teams in our pipeline, and the number of people accounted for on all those teams. Head count is an important metric that every manager understands. Most important, this slide included our desired footprint three years from now, in their division, with a year-by-year road map to hit that number.

Slide four was where most of the discussion occurred in our one-on-ones. We'd briefly discuss each team that was already in, and how they were doing. We'd discuss the teams scheduled and approved, and the pipeline. We'd also look at the human footprint growing inside their organization and talk about the reskilling going on and any new hiring they'd need to approve, even if down the road a bit. Provoking *that* dialogue was the primary design goal of the deck; we wanted the focus to be on the *future* and the *requirements to making that future happen*. The deck seemed exceedingly simple, even simplistic, but it was designed to generate maximal conversation with the precious time we had together—as opposed to piling on information.

I'm always mindful of how easily PowerPoint can be misused. People will put dozens or hundreds of bullet points into a slide deck and then try to talk over it. If you're intent on just vomiting information like that, maybe you should just put it in a memo and skip the meeting.

But in our case, it was never simply about regurgitating data. We needed to move our management as much as we needed to move the teams. In any transformation you have to change leadership as much as the followership.

So there was massive value in the personal interaction with the various senior leaders. Over time, they would believe, as Doug's point six foretold. But their belief would be borne from a trusting relationship developed during these conversations just as much as from the data.

The objective of the one-on-ones was to nudge these managers toward making the right choices in their fall plan. Because we couldn't be certain of any executive's genuine commitment to change, we purposely avoided pushing for answers on these calls. I've found that when any buyer gives you an answer of no, it's almost impossible to get them to change. Whereas, if they don't put themselves on the record with a no, then you've always got a chance. In our case, if one of our buyers seemed noncommittal, we could always engage Robert to help in the background.

Executing on this new approach made a few things very clear to us as we moved into the fall planning season for year two. We learned that these executives were very informed about the business outcomes each of their Hallmark teams were generating. They understood the general costs involved in running the teams, and they absolutely knew their revenues, market share, and overall business trajectory.

What they lacked, however, was any grasp of the *operational* aspects of the teams—for example the skill set and band-level makeup of each team, or the specific subskills missing or overloaded. That was information that existing management systems weren't providing, which would be fine if things were going well, but Hallmark existed because things had not gone well. When the times call for change and new ways of working, teams need their leaders to understand the specific operational challenges of change. This would become even more evident to us in our work unlocking the mystery of the shit umbrellas, but early on we knew that this data was required to motivate investment decisions at the very top.

Because we were so deeply involved in the operations of each Hallmark team, even with our simple slide deck as a guide, we found ourselves in deep discussions with GMs, going over issues they were not exposed to anywhere else. For example, they welcomed our opinions on the outdated tools that teams were being forced to use. We had some lively conversations about the importance of introducing new tooling, and we'd exit those meetings knowing that the GMs would raise this issue with their peers. All of these conversations contributed to the new culture we were trying to drive into the company. These meetings also gave specificity to Hallmark's claims of change and success, making it something worth investing in.

This new, more structured quarterly communication helped us in countless other ways. It reinforced the growing footprint of Hallmark both across IBM and inside specific people's portfolios, and it gave us leverage for other discussions, as well. For example, having briefed a divisional SVP and getting no pushback on our desired expansion, we gave ourselves permission to go directly to that division's chief financial officer (CFO) and check to make sure the next year's Hallmark team expenses were included in the upcoming fall plan. With this implicit SVP support, instead of getting stonewalled by "We can't afford all that travel for 20 teams" we would often get a more agreeable, "Okay, we may not be able to onboard 20, but we can give you 10."

In a similar way, discussions with leadership about tooling gave us the leverage to go to the information technology group, which owned tools (and their procurement) across IBM and say, "we covered with this SVP the need for Slack for their Hallmark teams. Would you let us pilot that?" The answer would usually be yes, because they didn't want to get in a fight with an SVP over such a small thing. We had learned in our early months that while we'd never win a battle to quickly get IBM to change entire toolsets, we could get the tools we needed in pilot mode here and there. This helped us move faster. Instead of waiting years for full secure global implementations, we could easily wall off teams here and there and use the new tools, at least for communications and data that wasn't confidential. This shaved quarters, if not years, off introducing new and much needed tooling upgrades for our teams.

Closing the Sale Doesn't Always Mean Getting Paid

The sharpened focus for each meeting increased our effectiveness in engaging with IBM's leadership. While each of our quarterly calls were scheduled for 15 minutes, as I recall, none of them ever stopped there. They always went for at least 30 minutes, and oftentimes even past that mark.

As senior leadership's interest grew in getting new Hallmark teams admitted, we would close the sale, letting them know about the cost ($60K to $120K per team), and that we would work with their CFO to make sure the agreed costs were included in the fall plan. This worked pretty well, right up until it didn't!

Several times in year two we were blindsided by budgeting red tape. More than once, we found out on a Friday that the bootcamp team due to arrive in Austin on Monday hadn't received final funding approval. The expense had been approved and reapproved right up to the previous month. Then, on Friday, while expecting the transfer of funds to go through, we learned the product team's business unit was under a temporary expense ban, or some other reason opaque to everyone but the CFO.

The budget process at IBM had a lead time of up to 18 months from first budget request to the release of funds—but those funds could always be modified or withheld in the internal accounting. Early in this process, while we were still running bootcamps, $100,000 might be budgeted to get a new team flown into Austin for their bootcamp, but maybe only $40,000 would be released. We'd have to scramble to cut back on the number of team members attending, or, perhaps, PH would make deals that split the difference: if they'd pay for half, he'd commit Hallmark to cover the rest.

Those budget fights were gritty and real, and when a project team leader took on the added burden of having those battles with their finance team, it made their own resolve and commitment to the program even deeper. And for the finance people, seeing their peers fight for inclusion in Hallmark made an impact on them. They learned that this Hallmark thing was highly valued and worth fighting for. Ironically, our relationships across the CFO organization grew out of these initial fights, and those relationships proved invaluable as we gained trust in one another. They learned the details of why the Hallmark Bootcamps weren't extravagant boondoggles, while we developed an appreciation for how often they'd been left in the dark about the timing of this expenditure until the last minute. If we could give them earlier visibility, they could plan better, and we'd both be happier.

Throughout this year two cycle of meetings, we'd advanced in our own understanding of our buyers, and we'd been successful in quadrupling the footprint of the program, adding 25 teams who paid for the privilege of joining the Hallmark program. But the implications of continued exponential growth over the coming years in head count, travel cost, content development, and above all funding, led to the realization we needed another leap in capability.

First and foremost, we needed more consistency in the funding. We could negotiate last minute changes and even reschedule when we were adding 25 teams in year two. It was a struggle, but doable. However, for 75 or 100 teams in year three? No way. The scheduling demands and the need for efficiency and scale simply wouldn't allow for that level of uncertainty.

Conditions also had changed. With more than 30 teams operational and a pipeline stuffed with scores of applications from new teams, we no longer had to pussyfoot around the finance issue. If you wanted in, you had to get your execs and your CFO aligned from day one. We didn't ask anyone to sign contracts, but we did set up email chains that included everyone who could possibly throw a wrench into the works. That way we secured a record of everyone's explicit financial commitments to fund the team, essentially at the date of admission.

Also, in order to achieve that level of scale, our simple deck and quarterly sessions were in need of another upgrade. With so many teams to run, we needed a real management system.

A System of Record for Change

Again, I turned to Doug for his thoughts on the matter. His response was that our existing deck format, already familiar to us and IBM's senior leadership, would be the perfect template on which to base a much more professional and information-rich management system tool. While retaining its ease of use, Doug transformed the deck into a new system of record that would help us continually marshal resources for Hallmark teams.

This new management tool included notes for each Hallmark team on their qualitative project outcomes, including analyst quotes and customer endorsements of Hallmark team products. They were accompanied by red/yellow/green assessments made by my leadership team and the psychiatrists to make it easy to flag teams that were underperforming. One visualization showed the career level of designers on their teams, and it would empirically show the imbalance among certain skill sets. All this new detail assisted in raising the level of conversation in our quarterly one-on-ones.

For example, one chart showed the shape of a skill set within a team—the number of people at each career band level. It would be clear when a project was lacking, say, experienced designers in the mid-career categories. Another visualization showed the various badged skills. Our conversation pivoted from us hollering about the need for more people into a more productive discussion about "how do we make the shape of this team better, so that each individual can make the maximum impact?" It was the kind of conversation that most managers could get on board with. With time we discovered that giving the managers a specific target shape to hit by the end of the coming year helped them integrate promotions and outside hiring more easily into their plans. It also prompted healthy skills-based conversations as opposed to career levels, something Ginni was keenly interested in.

As our metrics showed more of the direct impact on each manager's business outcomes, the quarterly meetings shed their prior informality and became much more professional. We became partners in business strategy, asking questions like, are all your most important projects in here? Which teams should be in Hallmark that aren't? And, likewise, are there teams no longer important enough for Hallmark's ongoing attention?

In the far-right columns were the number of designers and badged design thinkers, coaches, and advocates assigned to each project. Inevitably, a zero in one of these areas next to an important project would catch the manager's eye. "Are you serious?" the GM would say. "That's our absolute can't-lose project! That needs to change." A productive conversation ensued about optimal ratios, career levels required for assignment to that project, and next steps.

We included these detailed measures of how each division ranked in, say, awarded badges versus its peers, knowing that no one wanted to fall into the bottom half of Hallmark's metrics. By year four, the deck included the net promoter scores we'd collected on projects developed by Hallmark teams. At a glance, managers could see for the first time how customers were grading the products in their area of responsibility and connect the dots from that to the detailed skills makeup of each team. We didn't have to sell; the data spoke for itself.

It's important to understand that until Hallmark started generating these quarterly reports, IBM executives never had this level of insight into how product teams were staffed. They knew their team head counts, but much of the data we showed them had been managed below them with little or no information rising upward to their level. Hallmark's management system provided IBM's middle and upper leadership with standardized, consistent team data reporting they had needed for a long time. By providing new tools for change, we introduced IBM leadership to a more engaged and educated relationship with the new work culture.

Embedding Change in the Executive Ranks

From the first days thinking about the program and IBM's decentralized culture, I'd believed that in order for deep cultural behaviors to stick over time, it was critical that executives at both the SVP and GM levels have people *on their team* who ran design *for their team*. These would be the folks sitting on leadership teams across IBM business units facing the same challenges every other executive with domain expertise faced. They would be accountable for both design outcomes and business results, which helped cement design and design thinking as core business capabilities rather than just a creative function. But, again, there was no mandate for this.

We needed to design our management system to lead the user—the GM and the SVP—to the obvious, data-based conclusion that executive design leadership was needed in their division.

As we had those quarterly discussions, it was right there in the data that the numbers of people on Hallmark teams grew—people with design and design thinking skills. As we discussed the future, we always dealt in road maps over the next three years. The ramp of teams, the ramp of design thinking and agile practitioners, and the shape of those skill sets in terms of experience. To lead all this, I would observe, they might want to consider having dedicated design executives inside their business unit.

I told them, only half joking, "If you have your own design leader, it means you don't have to listen to me anymore." I say half-joking because one aspect of the autonomy granted to IBM business units was that GMs liked to have their own people, their own CFO, their own head of engineering. I was suggesting each of the GMs should also have their own heads of design and design thinking. It was one of many ways we hacked IBM's cultural predispositions to serve our mission. We helped by identifying and nurturing internal leaders who had managerial potential, and in parallel, we began attracting seasoned design executives from outside IBM who had experience scaling design organizations.

By the summer of year three, we had a network of senior design leaders embedded across our business units. Each executive had real authority and a seat at their division's leadership table. Each ran scores of designers and also owned responsibility for the division's Hallmark team staffing and management system. They hired. They fired.

The number of design executive positions almost naturally multiplied with the rapid growth of IBM's hiring of designers, because IBM management and budget culture assumed an approximate 100-to-1 ratio of executives to employee head count.

The role of the Hallmark program shifted yet again to one in which we introduced the new design leaders to their respective business units, while helping senior leadership manage their new capability. Most of these designers were brand-new to executive leadership and had no prior relationship with their respective GMs. We used our quarterly management system calls to help build these relationships, using the components of the management system as the agenda for these meetings.

The first time we conducted these rounds of meetings, Doug and I were fairly nervous. This was a new thing we were doing, and we were sensitive to how hard it might be for these two very different types of people to work together. Any misstep on the part of a newly appointed executive would not only be problematic for them but also for all the future executives we needed in place across the company. Word travels fast at those senior levels, and we wanted all the words to be good!

Executive leadership is fundamentally about resource allocation, which was a new responsibility for many of these people. Prior to each meeting, we spent time coaching the design leader to provide specific goals and targets—and not to preach the benefits of their profession. "Here's my plan for Hallmark team growth for the next three years." Or "let's consolidate design to these four locations over the next year." Then, for the initial meetings, Doug and I took very active roles in in the conversation, coaching, nudging the conversation along. With time, we were able to lean back and let the design leader guide the discussion. The more appropriate role for Doug and me was to contribute our knowledge about what was happening with design elsewhere across IBM.

The common language we'd brought to the management system enabled us to move on this highly distributed process of management change much more quickly. The result was not just a larger design organization but also a fundamentally different organization, one with new voices in leadership who could be relied on to champion the new ways of working until they were no longer new, but simply the way work is done at IBM.

Vertical Progression

The course of expansion in the design management ranks mirrored the progression of Hallmark teams through IBM's vertical divisions. We had started in our most strategic product divisions, then expanded next to IBM Services, before spreading across almost all of the rest of the divisions.

This gradual movement took a very deliberate path in a way that appealed to my entrepreneurial sensibilities. Most successful startups focus on a single strong vertical because it's easier to replicate your solution in a vertical and then achieve economies of scale. In Hallmark's case, the product teams were the natural starting points for reasons cited previously: they are stable, long-lived groups that have time to experiment and then truly embed new practices.

But soon we would move into our services organization, which had a unique risk–return quotient. It was riskier because of the teaming situation of a services organization. A person on a services team will be with a client for some short duration, and then they're going to break apart, and that team won't really stay together. It would take us a couple of years before we felt confident enough in the practices, and also had the scale of adoption, to approach our services organization and begin embedding design thinking and the studio culture.

Scaling up in this order was consistent with an IBM concept called *client zero*. IBM is so big that it will typically do things for itself for some period of time (sometimes months, sometimes years) before taking that new method or product to clients. Everything we learned about design thinking through our work with the first product teams eventually made its way into IBM's array of service offerings.

Of all the IBM business verticals, sales was kept for last because, well, it's much harder to develop the resolve to risk sales to unproven methods. But once our practices and tools were extremely robust, it was time. Two of our most experienced design leaders would tackle this effort: Karel Vredenburg and Nigel Prentice. Karel was a long-time IBMer with vast experience across all IBM units, including leading the Hallmark charge into services, and Nigel had led the psychiatrist team for years. Their pilot with four of our top sales teams yielded such impressive results that Karel and Nigel were able to build out a team to activate a new sales approach for each of our top 60 account teams globally.

This progression from products to services to sales represents what I consider a replicable and sustainable model for scaling change anywhere. It demonstrates how to use the risk profile of each vertical to prioritize the course of implementation. While products was our most profitable area, and therefore might be deemed "riskiest," it was in fact more suited to the changes. Long-lived teams working on well-defined projects. We were able to work in this environment to solidify our change provocation to a certain level. Then to services, which was riskier. Projects were shorter lived, and teammates were mixed and matched frequently. The provocation solidifies even more. And then with sales, the riskiest of all due to its direct impact on short-term results, you take the offering in its most mature state.

Unity, Not Uniformity

This evolution of management systems, design executives, and cross-vertical rollout was crucial to sustainable transformation. Our mission of achieving a sustainable culture of design thinking needed much more than thousands of designers. It needed distributed execution and governance operating at the highest levels of IBM.

During year four, at the height of Hallmark's influence, we began downsizing the centralized program team, by design. The design leaders across the various divisions of IBM were picking up more and more of the workload previously done by my team. Our intention was never to build a permanent program office. Sustainable change in today's highly decentralized world is only secured when change agents are distributed in positions of power throughout the organization, no longer measured by their success at the rate of change but by the business results of their units.

The alternative approach, through the centralized structures I see organizations frequently adopt for design, Agile, artificial intelligence (AI), and other capabilities are prone to two key pitfalls for which I've never seen an effective remedy:

- The group is given some fragile hold on power from the top, but it probably moves too slowly and gets in the way of the agile, distributed decision-making required at the edges of the organization.
- The group doesn't even really have that support at the very top and is always struggling to get the resources required and, ultimately, folds.

In modern organizations, it's a fact of life that any and all centralized functions—no matter how worthy—are oftentimes seen as burdens of dubious value. "I'm from corporate, I'm here to help," doesn't inspire confidence. Executives under extreme profit-and-loss pressures will always tend to perceive these programs as freeloaders, surviving only through the grace of the corporate dole. That's why "centers of competency" and other centralized programs are always one CFO pen stroke away from death, one bad quarter where their elimination helps the organization meet its numbers. That's true for design, for Agile, and, increasingly, for AI programs.

During one of my visits to Savannah College of Art and Design, I met with Tom Hardy, a professor and former IBM designer, who personally experienced IBM's once-great centralized design department quickly collapse from such brittleness.

Back in the 1960s and 1970s, IBM products and packaging were some of the best designed on the planet; it had perhaps the greatest constellation of designers ever assembled. However, the status of the department relied almost entirely on the special working relationship legendary designer Eliot Noyes enjoyed with CEO Tom Watson Jr. The design program had a lot of power as long as that relationship was in place. But Watson retired for health reasons in 1971, and Noyes passed away in 1977. Then, as many multinationals did at the time, the architecture of corporate governance shifted. The modern global corporation arose, with more power ceded to each local market, giving those executives in far-flung countries more control over how the company showed up. Of course, this included the design of packaging and product. Local fads were embraced, and the brand guidelines coming from US-based corporate were ignored. The centralized IBM Design Program would die a quick death.

This story had a great impact on me, and it informed my response to every aspect of our program architecture from the protein spikes to the embedded executives. The culture of design had returned to IBM, but in this incarnation, it is a sustainable culture worked into the sinews of everyday work throughout the global organization. Unlike the days of Noyes and Watson, design leaders at IBM don't report to any central design program or department. They have solid-line relationships to their business unit leaders so that each business unit can develop design responses to their specific needs and challenges.

But, although nothing formal was ever put in place, in practice these individuals also maintain what I call *virtual dotted-line relationships* to the design community so that they can maintain connection to the broader design system. We managed IBM Design thereafter like a community of shared values in which the members could rely on each other as learning resources. Karel Vredenburg from my team chaired a new IBM Design Leadership Board, although our role was more that of a community organizer and not a community leader.

The executives throughout the organization and the Leadership Board became extremely important to me. In a very real way, they replaced the Hallmark teams as my most leveraged point of contact with what was happening in the business. My continuing conversations with the SVPs and GMs were more and more about things I was hearing from their design leader or on coaching they could give their new design leader.

Of all of the program outcomes we achieved, I am proudest of the fact that today the executive ranks at IBM include dozens of design executives spread across the company and around the world. They don't do things identically to one another; they optimize for their groups and locales. To borrow the words of Eliot Noyes, they represent "unity, not uniformity." What unites them is their unbending support for this new culture, guaranteeing it will endure until the day a new and better way of working comes along.

Takeaways

- **Adjust the business model as demand and maturity grow:** Implement a phased funding approach that begins by offering change for free, then quickly transitions to charging for access as demand builds. Financial commitment demonstrates value and fosters accountability for program teams and leadership.
- **A great management system is your best sales tool:** Create a data-driven management system that gives executives unprecedented visibility into team composition, skill distribution, and performance metrics. This visibility helps them connect business outcomes to team structure while stimulating healthy competition through peer comparisons that drive further investment.
- **Decentralize leadership:** As you mature, embed dedicated leadership for the change initiative within each business unit, creating a decentralized network of accountable executives who own both the transformation and its business outcomes. This structure ensures the change survives beyond any central program office, making it resilient to organizational shifts.

9

Building
the Environment

In the months leading up to the Hallmark program launch in 2013, even among supporters I faced considerable skepticism as to whether the program I was recommending could scale across the entire organization.

"What's your formula?" asked one senior executive during a high-level committee briefing. I had to admit I couldn't answer off the top of my head.

The executive posing the question was Steve Mills, an icon of the technology industry who'd been with IBM since the early 1970s. Steve had built IBM's software business—and much of the modern software industry—from scratch. As IBM's sole executive vice president at the time, he started drilling me on the issue of scale, asking whether I understood it, and how we could measure progress at mastering it. He wasn't antagonistic but was genuinely trying to understand—and get me to understand—how to measure our impact in the early days in a way that might indicate probable success at a company of 400,000.

When he asked me "What's your formula?" he explained that it is impossible to scale a solution with constantly bespoke behaviors. Change at scale would require repeatable and measurable behaviors. It is the successful and repeatable application of a specific formula that indicates a program's maturity in terms of scale.

Flying back to Austin after that meeting, my mind turned to the question: what *is* our formula? And equally important, how do we ensure the formula doesn't become a simplistic checklist of tactics (which is a tendency at big organizations)? We needed something enduring regardless of the tactics used; no plan survives first contact with the enemy, as they say. Our formula had to be specific enough that it could be tracked, so that everyone could evaluate its progress, yet flexible enough that tactics could shift as needs changed.

What were the elements that, if applied over and over again, team by team, would most probably result in achieving our mission? I thought about culture itself, and cultures of the past. If I could define the levers of culture, I could perhaps conceive of a formula to hack IBM's.

It all started with outcomes. It was critical that our program be understood on the basis of the improved outcomes we achieved. We needed to change our culture to change our outcomes.

I thought about how anthropologists might understand the outcomes driven by some past culture. They'd look at the food, the art, and the work artifacts of the civilization, the structures built, and the tools created to build them. They'd study the geography and geology to determine the raw materials seen and unseen that shaped the people. They'd walk inside the shelters that were used, both the permanent housing and perhaps how the people lived while on the move. Working backwards, they would determine what skills the people obtained, as well as the processes they used in making their artifacts. Together, these would define a culture. The bones. The art. Weapons. Their skills and practices. Their homes and environment.

The next day in my office in Austin I went to the whiteboard and kept iterating on these thoughts. Writing down all the things that my anthropologist would be looking at, and then finally grouping the various things into categories. The people. Their activities. Their environment. I kept staring at that, and then at the top of the whiteboard I wrote the following:

CULTURE = OUTCOMES

Then,

CULTURE = PEOPLE + PRACTICES + PLACES

And then, finally,

PEOPLE + PRACTICES + PLACES = OUTCOMES

Here was our formula.

For the next several years as we scaled our program across cities and continents, this was the lens through which I communicated our progress. These would be the levers I pulled, and everything my team did was always checked against whether they were the most impactful things we could do, at any given point in time, to move one of these levers.

People, practices, and places, I reckoned, were deeply interdependent. Culture is a three-legged stool only as strong as its weakest leg. You can't expect to ignore one or two of them and achieve your change goals.

And yet, I've never seen a change program that included changing the very nature of *places* as a part of the transformation.

The Problem with Places

Any built environment tends to reflect the builders' values and reinforce the legitimacy of the status quo. IBM's engineering-driven, inward-facing culture found its expression in IBM places, as well. The group that managed work environments at IBM established standards that valued status, control, and ritual, while subordinating employee engagement and creativity.

When I was new to IBM, it baffled me why the Austin campus architects chose to design the hallways of our building to run along its glassed-in exterior. Then one day someone in our real estate group explained it to me: "If one person got a window, everyone would want one."

This windows policy was pursued to bizarre ends. When our whole Lombardi team was relocated to the IBM campus, I submitted a request to use some of our allocated integration funds to knock down the office walls on our floor. We all wanted and needed the same kind of open collaborative office space we were accustomed to at our former home. IBM's finance department approved the expenditure, but at the last minute the real estate office shot it down. Why? I was told that the open floor would mean we'd all have "window offices." IBM's no-windows culture had the last word.

The IBM physical plant did nothing to support who we were as people or how we wanted to work. If you had a private office, it was mandatory to lock your door when you left, which left miles of closed-door interior hallways that were drab gray and fluorescent lit (with only about 9 out of 10 lights working). Trash cans and occasional rubber plants were the only visual "stimulation." This not only failed to foster the collaboration modern work requires but also it alienated people to the point that, forget collaboration, they didn't even want to come into the office. It was depressing.

This experience was just one of many that impressed on me how the physical plant and the values it reflects influences the culture within. The work environment might seem tangential to work outcomes, but an alienating depressing environment has an undeniable impact on behavior—like all the "shushing" of us Lombardi people. I was convinced that bringing new people and new practices to IBM would go to waste if we couldn't provide new places that supported our culture shift toward faster and better outcomes.

The Austin Studio: Our First Experiment

Because of all this, I fought for our year one funding to include money (and the real estate group's preapproval!) to build a prototype space that would challenge many of the existing culture's precepts and reinforce the new ways of work. We were allocated an entire floor of one of the buildings on the Austin campus, but it would take almost a year for the planning and build-out, so we were given some temporary quarters.

The temporary space was a poor reflection of our hopes for the program. What we were given was an abandoned executive briefing center in a building off the main campus that would soon be sold. Our quarters were pretty much like my previous experience: there was a long hallway with one big room and two smaller rooms (although we did have a small kitchen). These were again lit with old school fluorescent lights and the gray walls of before, but with the lovely addition of heavy traditional boardroom furniture bolted to the floor (unnecessarily, since it all weighed a ton). But something remarkable happened in those temporary quarters. Our new designers, rather than accepting the constraints of the space, began actively reshaping it to meet their needs.

Adam Cutler was the senior designer on my Hallmark leadership team who was in charge of the new studio's plans, and he was also responsible for making the new space perform in the interim. He arrived one day to discover that half a dozen of the new employees had disassembled some of the massive boardroom tables and reconfigured the workspace in surprising ways! The next week, because their team was working on a very different problem, they'd taken the furniture apart and moved it around, yet again.

This pattern—the physical space shifting along with the context of a team's work—would repeat itself over and over. As the context changed, the built environment wanted to be changed to support it. Adam learned from watching how they worked, and it fundamentally shaped our approach to the permanent studio.

Adam set out a series of important design criteria for a fluid, open workspace, now informed by what he'd learned. The strategic design of the studio wasn't anything new: open, collaborative spaces have been in and out of fashion time and again. But what he'd unlocked was a new design point: all furnishings—tables, chairs, everything—had to be able to be moved easily, all the time. Tactically, it meant that everything possible must be on wheels. Anything not on wheels needed, we decided, to be light enough so that it could be moved easily by two people no taller than five feet tall and weighing no more than 100 pounds each. And no tools required. The finished product would be a workspace where everybody had the ability to sculpt and manipulate their environment quickly and easily to fit their ever-changing needs.

The insight here is that our transformation's goals were used to drive how our physical environment should exist, as opposed to leaving space design to a group unattached to the culture you intend to influence. In our case, we were moving from a siloed, hierarchical style of work to one that valued agility and the rich, interdisciplinary conflict that would drive better outcomes. Our spaces needed to not only reflect but contribute to that flexibility. In other contexts, the changes to place will likely be different, but no less important or profound—and should be driven by the change agenda, not some predefined criteria divorced from the goals of your program.

Place as Propaganda

Physical spaces also offered us a branding opportunity for our change product. The space could be a billboard promoting and encouraging our people in almost subliminal ways. In our case, we didn't use traditional IBM real estate branding, color, wall, or furniture options, but we did celebrate IBM. On the walls lining the space were images reflecting IBM's storied design legacy, with images of iconic IBM designers Eliot Noyes, Paul Rand, Charles and Ray Eames, plus that of legendary IBM CEO Thomas J. Watson, who famously said that "good design is good business." One way Hallmark legitimized design thinking at IBM was by claiming to restore the company's status as a design leader, which had been lost decades earlier as IBM exited nearly all its consumer product lines. Other walls were massive corkboards, inviting work artifacts to be pinned up and shared for feedback or just to show off.

The new studio was beautifully done but with none of those gimmicky flourishes you see in some workplace designs, like half of a VW bus sticking out the wall. This isn't what motivates people. Working with other smart people and engaging in authentic dialogue is what inspires us. It was modern, but it was a place where good work was the star.

Above all we wanted the work to be more precious than the place. We didn't want the space to dictate outcomes; we wanted the desired outcomes to shape the space. We let people more or less fill in the blanks for themselves, do what makes sense to them, which fostered their sense of belonging and shared ownership of the space, and produced a willingness to defend the shared values.

We also made choices that guaranteed a certain level of what Adam liked to call *intentional serendipity*. The spaces were designed to force interactions. When you exited the elevator bank, for example, we closed off what had been direct access to the kitchen area. We wanted people to be forced to walk the long way around, through the studio, where they would encounter people and work artifacts from other teams, many of whom they'd never met before. That was one of the simpler choices we made in floorplan design, where the other way would have been more efficient but less supportive of our cultural aims.

Authentic work culture transcends purely transactional spaces. This became clear when one Thursday I was approached by two of our new graphic designers who told me that a local print shop was selling off their old equipment and asked if we could buy it. I was caught off guard; I didn't have a clue what kind of equipment a print shop had. But it sounded like a crazy enough scheme that I sort of laughed and asked, "Well, are we talking $500, $5,000, or $50,000?" They hemmed and hawed and said, "maybe about $5,000." I said that that was at least in the realm of possibility and laughed, then went on my way.

The next Monday I came in and was shocked at the sight of a giant screen-printing press set up with a 10-foot stretch of wire drying racks! I tracked the two down and asked, "What's up with this?" They said that since I'd approved the spend, they bought the shop out over the weekend and moved the equipment in. What could I do but laugh? To this day I've got no clue how they moved that equipment in so fast or even got it to fit in the elevators. (I do remember the process of getting that expense approved; or I should say that my chief financial officer does!)

As it happened, that press drew in people from all over the campus who wanted to see it and try it. From all across the Austin campus engineers, finance folks, marketers, IBMers with no connection to Hallmark other than being in Austin were now in the space, attending one of the Thursday night poster-making classes and soaking up the new atmosphere. Most who'd never known what screen printing entailed found that it was fun and satisfying to make something by dragging a squeegee through a slab of ink and over the screen. In the spirit of maker culture, the rule sprang up that you could get a lesson on the press if you promised to teach the next person how to do it.

The screen printing turned out to be one of those things that visitors were enchanted by. When groups and clients came to Austin and visited the studio, they would often go home with their own custom-made posters commemorating their visit. But the utility of these and other features of the press isn't really the point of why I liked having the press.

These and other activities in the studio that were not directly productive and outcome-oriented were nonetheless fundamental to our making change irresistible at IBM. They demonstrated the transformational impact of play and creativity on the culture. They were instruments of change, not mere by-products of it. They weren't passively "cool"—like the VW bus— they were cool only because they actively engaged people, which signaled change and our new interdisciplinary way of working.

One day Adam sat with his team to discuss their places, priorities for the next six months and Miroslav Azis said out of the clear blue, "I want to make a radio station." Adam's practical side had a hard time seeing the business impact of IBM Radio and it struck him as also a potential copyright minefield. But Miroslav persisted that he just thought people in the studio would enjoy spinning music for each other.

Some front-end developers using open-source frameworks built the station—IBM Community Radio!—with very little trouble. People in the studio could sign up and schedule half-hour blocks to play their favorite music.

And, like almost every good idea, it exploded… globally. Expanding way beyond just music, there were call-in shows, podcast-type interview shows with Hallmark leaders, discussions about design and emerging technologies. One program interviewed many of the most senior IBM leaders to tell the stories and lessons of their own careers. Ginni herself sat in for two lengthy interviews over the years.

The station was accessible to everyone behind the IBM firewall, and it wasn't long before IBMers in other time zones were requesting slots for their programming. In November 2016, *Fast Company* magazine published a story, "IBM's Unlikely Silo Buster: An Intranet Radio Station." Miroslav told the magazine, "This has really flattened the organizational structure. You meet people in other organization silos."

There were so many cultural cues built into the studio that it went far beyond the objective of injecting design thinking into IBM. We wanted to challenge this behemoth corporation's sense of itself. The Austin studio was a home for our designers, but it wasn't their exclusive preserve. We made it clear that everyone on the IBM campus—and to visitors from beyond the campus—that everyone was welcome to come by, grab a cup of coffee, and pull up a couch. The work groups who chose to meet at the studio came from all across IBM—hardware, software, and services, but also from departments like marketing and communications.

Everyone took notice when a team from IBM's security products group started showing up at the studio. This team worked on software for the US military's special operations command, and within IBM, their work was the gold standard for smarts and seriousness—and they loved the studio.

They developed a new mantra for themselves: "Don't ship shit." This was prominently printed on dozens of notes and placards and posters that they tacked to one of those cardboard walls and, later, as a gift to their team leader, the team went out and had an eight-foot-by-five-foot blanket made with those words woven on it, and they hung it prominently in their space. It was exactly the kind of thing they couldn't do back at the office with the cubicles and locked doors and fluorescent lights. This was the spirit that began to take hold across Hallmark and, more and more, across IBM.

The Austin studio also helped alter the outside world's perceptions of IBM, especially after the *New York Times* article in 2015 revealed that IBM was working in the studio side-by-side with GameStop employees. I told the reporter from the *Times* that getting clients into the studio could help "fundamentally change their relationship with IBM," and it was true. More and more of our clients wanted to work with us in this place not because it was cool but because teams inside it generated faster and better outcomes.

Design thinking had evolved from an internal product development methodology to becoming central to how we transformed our clients' businesses. I was particularly proud of the introduction of IBM Garages as co-creation hubs where we could scale this side-by-side experience globally with our clients. What really got me excited about the garages was that Hallmark had nothing to do with them! IBM Garages didn't even include our core design teams in their development. They were started by engineers who saw the value of our new ways of work, developed their own vision, and ran with it.

It's hard to express what I felt seeing such a bold commitment to design by IBM engineers. I knew we'd crossed yet another threshold. This wasn't top-down change anymore—it was cultural transformation taking on a life of its own. Ginni's 2018 letter to shareholders gave a shout-out to the garages, reflecting how far we'd come in less than five years. She wrote, "Industry experts from IBM Services are co-creating cloud-enabled solutions with clients in our IBM Garages. Using design thinking and agile methods, we are helping clients implement new ways of working, such as rapid prototyping and iteration to more quickly move technology projects from pilot to production at scale."

That's the real power of corporate leadership in driving change: not by mandating new practices but, instead, by communicating at moments that spark virtuous cycles of adoption. The key is patience. Most change efforts use the bully pulpit too soon, burning through the CEO's credibility before the transformation has a chance to take root. Wait until you see signs of organic adoption, and that same influence becomes a powerful accelerant for change that's already in motion.

Place as Inspiration

The IBM Garages were only one instance in which the *people + practices + places* formula took on a spontaneous physical form. The new culture of place proved to be a natural extension of our program's irresistibility. As with the garages, we began to see something powerful with the studios themselves: change spreading through attraction rather than mandate.

When Gerhard Pfau came to Austin in 2013 for his team's Hallmark bootcamp, he was so inspired by his visit to the Austin studio that he returned to his IBM site in Böblingen, Germany, and rallied support for a studio there. It happened that the Böblingen campus, not far from Stuttgart, had a sizable group of senior IBMers who were also professional designers. One designer had started at IBM more than 30 years earlier, during the glory days of design guru Paul Rand. Gerhard led that group of designers (along with many non-designers from his team) to persuade IBM site management to build out a studio of their own. They were given a good-sized storage facility, one that had stashed a decade or more worth of broken furniture and obsolete computers. With a grant from their site fund of about €10,000, this group spent six months after-hours and on weekends building out a new studio, based on the design of our Austin studio.

At the time, I knew none of this. Then one day I received an envelope in the mail with a framed pair of scissors and a red ribbon, inviting me to Böblingen to help them open their "new studio." Alongside the plaque was a copy of the story I just told you. I was gobsmacked. The opening was a magical and emotional trip; at a campus halfway around the world, people I'd never met had funded and built a new studio on the force of one individual being catalyzed by an early bootcamp. Soon thereafter, I'd relate that story to the top 300 leaders at IBM and I'm not ashamed to say I choked up while telling it. I was incredibly affected by the passion and goodwill of those crazy Germans. I still am.

By year three, people at IBM sites all over world were clamoring for spaces that looked and felt like the studios in Austin and elsewhere. The same real estate office that rejected my request for an open floor plan in 2010 was greenlighting far more radical plans in the space of four years. The reaction was immediate and visceral. People wanted to be a part of something so dynamic. So much so that IBM's board of directors wanted to experience time in the new space, in Austin, and also get a feel for the activities of this new way of working. For only the second time in its history, the board met outside the company's headquarters, spending two days in Austin, one of which was a thorough tour and debriefing by my team and many of the Hallmark program team leaders. Shortly thereafter, the executive suite in Armonk, New York, IBM's headquarters, was redesigned, adopting many of the design cues of our design and agile workspaces. Senior leaders told me how surprised they were that the physical changes to their environment changed the way even the most senior people in the organization collaborated.

During the eight years from 2012 to 2020, more than 75 IBM Studios would sprout up all over the world, but more important, the agile workspaces adopted by the entire organization would use the same design language and lessons learned and cultural cues that our Austin studio prototyped and perfected. In total, IBM would invest more than $1 billion in improved real estate globally that reflected our new culture, engaging IBMers everywhere. But like everything at Hallmark, the culture change with places began as a one-at-a-time opt-in-only proposition.

Remote Is Also a Place

Now, the word I used, *places* was nicely alliterative in my formula, but places always meant more than the physical offices. Place, in my mind, certainly includes physical space but it's shorthand for something more like "the environment within which you work."

With all my emphasis on the physical components of our studios, it's easy to miss that much of the work at IBM is done via distributed teams, sometimes from all over the world. One challenge of workplace design is remembering that modes of remote work are aspects of place, and the customs of remote work should offer the same level of engagement for the people and the practices as any physical space. We found we needed to be more intentional about virtual settings that were required to serve the teams in delivering outcomes.

It was another case where we learned by watching employees using the tools for remote connection, and not always the tools we anticipated. Someone had bought a number of old, discarded IV stands from a medical supply place and then devised a little sling for each one so that an iPad could hang on the stands.

With that simple tool, our team members could do Facetime calls with teammates in other cities and adjust the height according to whether they were standing or sitting. We found that some would maintain that connection all day, just to have company and avoid the bother of calling or texting. Two people would be working as though they were side by side, and checking in with each other occasionally, showing each other a graphic or chart on the iPad and then going back to work. We'd never seen anything quite like it before.

The IV stands were put to work during the first Friends & Family Weekend at the studio. We held these because it's so important for everyone around us to understand the environment we're spending so much of our lives in. Anyway, the woman who headed the security product team gave her parents a remote tour, with their heads appearing on an iPad as she wheeled them around and introduced them to her team members. Another member of the team was doing the same for his parents, and there came a moment when it was time for the two pairs of parents to meet. The two team members rolled the IV stands toward each other until they were two feet apart, and their parents conversed as best they could, needing to pause for the uproarious laughter.

The deep experience we had with optimizing distributed teamwork meant that when the COVID-19 pandemic struck in March 2020, we didn't miss a step. Every one of our teams was fully prepared to work remotely because we'd already been operating well in distributed teams for more than six years.

Irresistible Places

The pandemic of 2020 changed everything about how we think about office work, but it didn't change human nature. People still crave connection, still want to feel part of something bigger than themselves. What changed was the burden of proof. Where once employees had to justify working from home, now leaders must justify why anyone should come to the office at all. And "because I said so" isn't cutting it.

I think about our Austin studio experiment differently now. We never had to mandate attendance—people wanted to be there. They came early, stayed late, and even brought friends and family with them. The security product team didn't camp out in our space because they had to; they came because something magical happened there that they couldn't replicate in their regular offices. When places nurture creativity and connection, you don't need policies to force attendance.

Today's leaders mandating return-to-office (RTO) policies are solving the wrong problem. They're focusing on attendance rather than engagement. If your people don't want to be in your space, that's not their failure—it's yours. The spaces you've created aren't compelling enough. Full stop.

Remember how our designers kept reconfiguring that massive boardroom table in our temporary space? They were telling us something important: spaces need to support how people actually work, not how we think they should work. When we built the permanent studio, we made everything movable because that's what our people needed. We watched, we learned, and we adapted. That's the playbook for today's hybrid world.

And here's the thing about hybrid work that many miss: it's not about splitting time between home and office. It's about creating environments—both physical and virtual—that make work better. Our security team working with special ops? They were almost never all in the same room. But when they were in our space, we made sure it supercharged their distributed collaboration. The IV stands with iPads weren't just cute hacks—they were deliberate tools to make remote teammates feel physically present.

The mandate shouldn't be "Employees: return to office." The mandate should be "Employers: create spaces so magnetic that people choose to come in." And when they do come in, the space needs to actively support their hybrid reality—great videoconferencing, quiet areas for virtual meetings, and technology that makes remote teammates feel present. Ironically, in today's world, if your physical office doesn't make virtual work better, you haven't built the right office.

I get so frustrated by management claims that mandated office time fosters "better collaboration" when most cross-functional teams are distributed across multiple locations. If meeting face-to-face is required for better collaboration, then why is it okay for teams to be distributed? It doesn't make sense. In studying post-pandemic work, I've started to think about collaboration differently.

The work we do with our teammates to get a job done is what I now call *transactional collaboration*. And let's be honest, most of this can be done extremely effectively via the video-conferencing and artificial intelligence (AI) tools that emerged from the pandemic, maybe even more effectively than the alternative. Leaders who are using the "better collaboration" argument for these situations are largely mistaken (or, perhaps, disingenuous).

The value of places is everything else.

At IBM, instead of focusing solely, or even mostly, on this transactional collaboration, we focused on other aspects of our culture that needed help: creativity, connection, morale, mentorship, accountability. Or in other words, active engagement for the betterment of someone's personal career, their work community, and their connection to IBM's mission. To do this, we built spaces that stimulated interaction via experiences that couldn't be accessed digitally. We intentionally made the physical place something that people *wanted* to be at.

For example, we had the typical global town halls across Hallmark once a quarter. These were broadcast across the company, recorded for later access, all the usual stuff. At the same time, I also started a tradition that we called the *Campfire*, which was a location-only meeting. Anyone could attend and I, or one of the Hallmark leaders, would hold a question-and-answer session that wasn't broadcast, and it wasn't recorded. We did this for one main reason: at Campfires, the conversation could be real and raw. It was a place where anyone could ask anything and be comfortable. When a campfire was held in a given location it was widely publicized in advance, and always well-attended. People want the inside scoop. At Campfires through the years, we tackled some pretty thorny topics, and people felt they were getting straight answers, even if they didn't particularly like them. Campfires became a must-attend event. No mandate.

We also spent a tremendous amount of energy connecting people to the physical spaces in other ways. One day two of our designers walked into my office and handed me a bound magazine. It was high quality but clearly handmade. About 30 or 40 pages, beautifully photographed and with well-written stories about the new IBM culture. It looked and felt like the original *Wired* magazines of the 1990s. I was impressed but didn't get what they were doing or wanted. So I asked, and they said it was a prototype of a magazine they'd like to start publishing. It would be a celebration of the culture we were driving at IBM. It would be a labor of love and would accept contributions from any IBMer in the world; but it would be curated and designed by a small group of highly talented graphic designers. It would always be quality.

I loved it! In about 30 minutes the three of us had estimated budget requirements and I approved the quarterly publishing. I only had two rules that they had to agree to. First: the magazine would only be analog; it would never be digital. And second: copies would be shipped to every IBM location, but only a few to each.

This wasn't just about creating a beautiful publication on heavy-stock paper. By limiting distribution and making it physically available only in our design studios and agile workspaces, we made the magazine's specificity of place part of its special nature. It became another thread in the fabric of our cultural transformation—not just through its content but also through how people had to engage with physical spaces to access it.

John Lennon sang about life happening while you're busy making other plans. At IBM, we learned that culture is what happens in the space between a team's transactional collaboration. Whether those spaces are physical or virtual isn't the point—it's whether they nurture the outcomes you need. If you're forcing people back to "hoteling" cubicle farms, you're not just failing to attract them—you're actively repelling them. And no policy in the world can fix that.

The solution isn't to strengthen the mandate. It's to take on the burden of irresistible change and apply it to your office culture. Make places that people value being in. Because when you build it right, like we did with the Austin studio, they don't just come—they engage!

Finding Your Formula

The impact to IBM's growing reputation for creativity was now viscerally communicated by the vibrancy of our workspaces. I was reminded of that when John Maeda, former dean of the Rhode Island School of Design, came to tour the studio.

John said to me, after he'd gotten a good look at everything, "This is a real design studio."

I was thinking, yes, of course it is. I had to ask him what he meant by that.

"Well," he said, "I see you've got these $3,000 Steelcase whiteboards here, and you've got plenty of them, and I know that your corporate budget paid for those things."

Then he pointed to all our other whiteboards, maybe 75 of them, made out of clothing racks, with whiteboards glued back-to-back and zip-tied to the frames. He said he was also impressed by the bikes hanging from hooks that had been similarly improvised.

"IBM gave you a space," he said "Your studio is what you built on top of it."

The *people* + *practices* + *places* = *outcomes* formula provided a comprehensive lens for culture change beyond the tactical change provocation. It showed that real change requires a holistic view, albeit one that can be scaled up relatively inexpensively to start.

This is the challenge facing leaders today as they wrestle with issues from AI to RTO. The answer isn't in mandating office hours or education, it's in creating an environment people want to be a part of because they are receiving personal value from it. There has to be a personal value proposition as well as the company's value proposition for any change to be authentically adopted.

It's true with people. It's true with practices. It's true with places. If you show just a few people a better way in each area, you will create demand for change that will grow to encompass your entire company.

Takeaways

- **Place is a foundational pillar of cultural architecture:** The value of spaces lies less in the *transactional collaboration* between teammates to get a job done and more about the broader, perhaps less tangible aspects of work life that inform those collaborations, which ultimately define a person's career and a company's culture.
- **Places should be magnetic, not mandated:** Places are the kitchen tables and living rooms of work, where *intentional serendipity* can have an outsized impact on your organization's culture and your people's careers. Mandates serve neither. Places should be curated with inviting content that is accessible only in person and that provide a personal value proposition to each person, as well as advance organizational goals.
- **Remote is a place, too:** Approach virtual and hybrid environments with the same intentionality as physical spaces. Digital interactions and rituals—whether from home or between campus locations—require deliberate design to ensure they reinforce the culture you are striving to create. The best physical spaces should also be the best places for remote connection.

10

Finishing the Job

Back in 2012, Ginni Rometty had asked what it would take to bring this new way of working to all of IBM's teams. My best guess at the time was that we would need to hire 1,000 designers over five years. But by the end of 2016, Hallmark's year four, we had 1,600 designers reporting to design executives inside every IBM division. We had far exceeded my initial expectations, and we'd done it faster than I'd thought possible.

Earlier that year, IBM had launched Cognitive Build, a massive, companywide AI project-building competition. Run from Hallmark's Austin Studio and hosted by Ginni and our chief brand officer Jon Iwata, it was part global science fair, part *Shark Tank*. The idea was audacious—any IBMer could form an interdisciplinary team to build an AI project. Qualifying teams were required to use Hallmark's way of working, which by now had simply become the IBM way of working. The winning team would get the funding necessary to turn their project into a real IBM product. More than a quarter million IBMers participated in the contest, forming 8,361 teams all over the world.

We had set out to make change go viral, and by 2016 it looked like we'd achieved it. A program like Cognitive Build was only possible because of how the new ways of working had infiltrated into vast global networks of expertise. By then, we had awarded more than 60,000 design thinking badges and had also credentialed hundreds of team-level Coaches and management-level Advocates—designations we hadn't even dreamed of until year three.

As the new way of work spread, it was accompanied by cultural values of creativity, self-expression, and initiative—all fairly novel concepts in the IBM I first experienced. I had begun challenging the teams new to Hallmark to go ahead and change their own spaces to accommodate the new practices they'd learned, like the folks in Böblingen. Don't wait for corporate to come along and do it for you, I told them. We even put in place incentives and competitions to encourage do-it-yourself studio building. (Example: "Phil will dedicate and run a global town hall from your studio if you build it.") New studio spaces in Dublin, Ireland; Hursley, United Kingdom; and Shanghai and elsewhere sprang up in response.

And at the same time, the change model designed to power Hallmark project teams found a much wider market throughout the IBM organization. The same principles that made change irresistible within our project teams also helped drive much-needed transformation in some of IBM's most entrenched functions.

The chief information officer (CIO) office at IBM became a powerful champion for change, partly out of our relentless requests for piloting newer and more capable software tools from the outside. By creating an entirely new IBM tool chain that supported our new way of working, the CIO office burnished its image within IBM as it shifted from that of gatekeeper to that of innovation enabler.

Even our legal and procurement functions, traditionally the most resistant to change of any organization, proved susceptible to the change virus. Our sales teams worked with key customers to develop new streamlined processes more appropriate to the speed and dynamism of modern work. Legal and procurement, to their credit, rose to the challenge and created new processes that were better for both IBM sales teams and for IBM clients.

In each instance, we spread change by following the same general formula that had made change irresistible to every Hallmark team:

- We started small and focused on willing partners.
- We demonstrated tangible value to create pull, rather than push.
- We made participation a privilege, not an obligation.
- We gave complete transparency into what was working and what wasn't.
- We allowed teams to adapt the approach to their specific context rather than enforcing rigid uniformity.

What I find most remarkable is how this pattern scaled from small product teams to even the largest of IBM's shared services. The fundamental dynamics remained the same, even though the mechanics differed widely. If you can show people practices that will improve their work life and provide them with agency in how they implement them, change becomes irresistible.

This is not to say it's always easy. When the work of our product teams was hampered by engineers with poor aptitude for creating user-friendly digital interfaces, we had to enlist support from human resources (HR) for changing how engineers were classified and evaluated. Because of our relentless focus on user experience, it became apparent that we needed to cultivate specialists in front-end software development, but the leaders of IBM's legacy engineering culture objected to classifying engineers that way.

It took countless meetings over two years before we could arrive at an agreement. Along the way, we used as evidence our deep knowledge of each team's design artifacts versus the coded outcomes, coupled with often dismal net promoter score (NPS) feedback from IBM software users forced to cope with poorly functioning interfaces. In such cases, the job of the change agent is to surface the fundamental misalignment between the systems and rituals of the old culture versus the requirements the new culture demands. You won't always have the power to change these systems on your own, and it's often a long, heavy slog converting key constituencies into allies—like HR in this case—to help battle with the people who can authorize the changes.

Sooner or later, these dynamics of principles of irresistible change will provoke change toward your new thing at every level of the organization. Whether you're transforming a 10-person team or a 10,000-person corporate division, the same human truths apply. Start with willing partners, show rather than tell, and stimulate demand for change by demonstrating success. You will help change go viral by enabling the organization's immune system to adapt rather than by trying to overwhelm it.

Beyond IBM

By year four, I was spending about half my time on the road. As less and less of the Hallmark work required my hands-on attention, the nature of my job shifted to helping drive growth for IBM. When IBM won a big services contract with a major petroleum company, I went to visit with their chief marketing officer (CMO) in London several weeks after work had begun. We met in the IBM London studio, where a fully integrated team of IBMers and our client's people worked in dedicated space marked off with our client's branding. The CMO so enjoyed the studio environment that he told me he was spending about one-third of his time there. He also confided that no one at the company ever expected IBM to win the bid. When the request for proposal was released, he explained, IBM was included as "column fodder." It was the London studio and the team's engaging way of working that won IBM the contract. It was completely at odds with their preconceptions about the company.

I heard similar sentiments from clients throughout North America, South America, Europe, India, Australia, and the Asia Pacific region. Not one person I met failed to be impressed by the breadth of IBM's transformation. Our open, online platform for IBM Enterprise Design Thinking enabled more than 250,000 non-IBMers, from companies all over the world, to be credentialed in design thinking the IBM way. In a very short time, IBM's client-facing garages and design studios would far outnumber the internal studios.

As our services organization began engaging with clients using the common language of IBM Enterprise Design Thinking, IBM's transformation attained another level, giving us new service offerings and providing better ways to engage across IBM's existing portfolio of services. Shortly thereafter, a study of both internal and external projects by Forrester would confirm what we were seeing at the time: at two-thirds of typical project costs, Hallmark-influenced client engagements were delivering faster and with better market results. The study would find that both employee engagement and retention levels had reached record highs for IBM.

After the CEO of one of our largest financial services clients flew his entire leadership team to Austin to see our studio, he sent Ginni an email that nicely summarized the state of our program at the time:

An approach like this will also be essential to building & implementing meaningful transformations that are made possible by the capabilities of Big Data & Analytics. At its core, [design thinking can help us] become more agile, and increase clock speed. When you think about IBM's big transformations, they involved changes in paradigms; from machines to computers, from hardware to software & services, and now from services & solutions to the very way people think & collaborate to solve foundational problems. IBM continues to be at the center of helping the world adapt.

Thanks to you and your team Ginni!

IBM's commitment to our users' experiences took a huge step forward in 2016 when the company acquired three design agencies in the United States and Germany. The acquisitions supercharged a part of our services group known as IBM iX, which grew rapidly to almost 20,000 consultants from only a few thousand in 2013. This unit, specifically charged with designing the human-centered systems of our clients, was the fastest growing part of our services business. None of these developments were driven by Hallmark, but all of them were powered by the Hallmark-developed design thinking toolkit.

When the organization begins spending millions buying up design agencies, it's reasonable to assume it might be time to declare the mission accomplished. It certainly raises this question about change: how do you know that you're finished? When can you be assured that the new culture is the new normal and the old culture is no longer compromising the quality of your outcomes?

Evidence was everywhere that the new way of working had suffused IBM. But the picture looked a little different regarding outcomes. It still didn't seem like IBM was experiencing the full benefits of change. After all, during each of Hallmark's first four years, IBM's revenues and net income fell. The company was shrinking in size with periodic layoffs necessary to reduce head count. Can you say you're done when that's still going on?

User reviews of IBM software had never been better, but those better-quality products had not moved the needle on sales. What was there left for me and Hallmark to do?

It was a mystery, tied to the related more general question of how do you know when your change program is completed. As it happened, we'd been working on the answer to both questions for several years.

We just didn't know it.

The Universal Experiences

One day during Hallmark's year two, while Charlie Hill and I were discussing the wide variabilities in team outcomes, we began questioning the nature of user experience itself. Charlie and I agreed that today's consumer culture extols the value of "great experiences," but as we dug into it, we found no agreement on what defines a great experience. More to the point, we couldn't come to any common understanding of how a user experience leads to any directed outcome. We had to admit that although design is devoted to improving user experience, the total experience of any product is very difficult to change because its use extends over so many varied touchpoints. All our teams had concrete evidence that they were "improving their users' experience," yet business results weren't changing.

I asked Charlie about his iPhone. What did he like best about it? He said he liked its ease of daily use. Only half-joking, I said that my favorite iPhone experience was opening the perfectly fitted box of a new iPhone and then finding the product inside, beautifully presented. After our conversation, I started asking around about what people like most about their iPhones. Some said it was the feel of the phone in their hands. Others said it was how the consistency in app design made it easy to learn a new app quickly. Still others told me it was the way it enabled their family's shared photo stream. That's when I came to realization that the daily experience of using a product—the central focus of almost all the work on the early Hallmark teams—is really only one part of any user's total experience with that product.

There seemed to be a universe of "experiences" with the iPhone that was as diverse as the number of people I asked. That was a serious problem. How could we ever systematically scale a method for improving user experiences if we couldn't concretely describe the specific experiences requiring improvement? Our mission to bring a sustainable culture of design thinking to IBM was in service of generating better outcomes that would affect sales and growth. We now needed a vocabulary or taxonomy that would enable us to design for and evaluate the total customer experience of each IBM product. We needed a framework that would enable us to surgically target the experiences that would improve specific outcomes needing attention for any given product.

IBM had thousands of products, so this at first seemed like an overwhelming task. I went to my whiteboard and started noodling. Slowly, I developed a classification system based on all the experiences people had told me about their iPhones. There were, I felt, a series of stages, common to all product experiences (as far as I could tell) that reflect how each product is experienced by its user. I showed this list to Charlie, and he agreed we should push on this thread and develop a defined system of a product's user experiences. If we could arrive at an agreed-on criteria for evaluating any given product across the full range of user experiences, we could assess our performance better and raise the overall quality of our work.

Months of research, discussions, debates, and negotiations ensued across the company. Finally, we settled on what became nine *universal experiences* that met the need of a user.

In any encounter with any product or service, there are nine distinct experiences that can be measured for customer satisfaction and then optimized:

- Discover
- Learn
- Try
- Buy
- First time use
- Everyday use
- Extend
- Get help
- End use

We found that while these nine experiences look very different in implementation, they are virtually identical in context across every possible product or service. For example, being confronted on eBay with images of bicycle saddles for sale and walking into a Walmart looking for a pain reliever are completely unrelated activities. But their context is identical. In both instances, you're trying to quickly discover something that fulfills a need. And from the retailer's perspective, in both cases they need to steer you effectively toward the thing they want you to want!

Similarly, getting stranded at an airport because of a missed connecting flight is very different from not knowing how to share an iPhone photo over Bluetooth, but the context—the user's mindset—is identical: "I need help."

This is the background for the universal experiences. It marks a fundamental shift in how we think about product development and go-to-market strategies, aligning each response and user solution on one of the corresponding contexts.

It's the first framework I've seen that offers a vocabulary for scaling empathy.

I particularly love *End use* because it's so rarely considered. But it's often one of the most powerful. Netflix, for example, delivers a great experience for this. When you cancel, you get a very thoughtful email letting you know that Netflix would like you to come back one day, and if you do it within the next 12 months, you will find all your data and preferences have been preserved. You've quit Netflix, but Netflix is ready to welcome you back over the next year with no consequences. Someone intentionally designed and built for that exceptional experience.

Great brands like Apple and Ritz-Carlton reliably deliver with excellence on all nine of these experiences, and that's the kind of company IBM should want to keep. We told our colleagues that when assessing the quality of a product, every one of these nine universal experiences needs to be thoughtfully considered by every function involved in the go-to-market: engineering, product management and design, marketing, sales, contracts, and pricing. Anyone who had any part in a user's experience of this product needs to be considered in its evaluation.

What this list revealed to me was that all over IBM, teams tended to over-index on *Everyday use* while ignoring the fundamentals for *Discover*, *Try*, and *First time use*. I could see the trouble this was causing, as less-capable software competitors were stealing market share from IBM because they'd made it so easy to be discovered, tried, and started with, even as their everyday features and value proposition were not as strong as ours.

For the first time, the focus of culture change moved beyond the narrow confines of product team excellence. By gathering NPS data on each distinct experience, we could now start assessing a given product or service across all the IBM departments and divisions contributing to that product's marketplace presence.

This level of rigorous corporate governance transformed our evaluation process from good/better/best qualitative assessments to concrete findings grounded in measurable metrics. As our products became increasingly cloud-based, we integrated real-time feedback mechanisms, such as pop-up surveys during product use, to capture immediate user experiences.

The universal experiences framework ultimately became our most powerful tool for transforming parts of IBM previously considered untouchable: our massive, shared service organizations.

The traditional challenge with functions like support, procurement, or legal is their scale and horizontal nature. These organizations serve thousands of products and typically operate with standardized processes that prioritize efficiency over customer experience. When customer satisfaction suffers, the typical approach is a company-wide mandate to "improve support"—a blunt instrument that rarely delivers meaningful change.

Michelle Peluso, our CMO, recognized the transformative potential of the universal experiences to solve this seemingly intractable problem. Rather than attempting to overhaul the entire support organization at once, she leveraged our framework to create surgical intervention points through product-specific accountability.

Here's how it worked: every quarter, Michelle convened the DUX (design and user experience) meeting to evaluate IBM's top 15–20 products across all nine experience categories. When a high-value product showed poor performance in, for example, the *Get help* experience, that specific product's support experience became a transformation priority—regardless of the overall support organization's performance.

This approach created a revolutionary dynamic. Support leaders couldn't hide behind organizational averages or cost-per-ticket metrics. Instead, they faced direct accountability for the experience of IBM's most strategic products. The conversations shifted from abstract discussions about support processes to specific customer journeys with measurable business impact.

One striking example: a flagship cloud product was showing strong growth but concerning renewal rates. The DUX review revealed its *Get help* experience scored dramatically lower than competitors. Rather than launching another overarching support transformation initiative, Michelle assembled a cross-functional team focused exclusively on transforming this product's *Get help* experience.

Within six months, the targeted intervention showed remarkable results. The product's *Get help* experience NPS rose 22 points, and renewal rates increased 9 percent. This success created internal demand—other product teams wanted the same focused approach to their support challenges.

The beauty of this model was its scalability through prioritization. We couldn't transform every support experience simultaneously, but we could systematically address the most strategically important ones first. This generated wins that built credibility and created internal pull for change. Support leaders, seeing the success, became partners rather than obstacles.

One senior vice president (SVP) captured this paradigm shift perfectly: "For 20 years, we've tried to fix support as a function and failed. This is the first time we've fixed it where it matters most—in the actual customer experience with our most important products."

We applied this same surgical approach across other traditionally resistant shared services:

- Legal processes for our top cloud offerings were streamlined while the broader contracting organization remained unchanged.
- Procurement cycles for key AI initiatives received special attention and resources.
- Billing and invoicing for strategic clients saw targeted improvements.

Each intervention created a proof of concept that could then be expanded methodically. By starting with the service experience product-by-product rather than function-by-function, we transformed areas previously considered too large and entrenched to change. In this way, we had the opportunity to elevate the shared service leaders to the status of strategic partners. They were now regarded as critical contributors to product success, rather than as cost centers. They gained a seat at the table in product strategy discussions because their metrics, once limited to per-caller efficiency, now shifted to that of customer impact.

This framework also facilitated the coordination among corporate marketing, product marketing, and product development teams. As successful patterns were identified for the top products, they could be replicated across numerous other products. We had a language that could in an instant align entire portfolios of products, entire lines of business, to optimize for an outcome in a given area—like discovery—in their next release.

One day an SVP commented to me in reference to the universal experiences, "This is literally the best thing you guys have produced."

He was right. We didn't appreciate it at the time, but this was Hallmark's crowning achievement. At some point we had accomplished all we could at team-level culture change. We had begun with the idea the team would be the atomic unit of change, and for three or four years it was. But by the end of year four, IBM teams were fully culturally transformed. There was no change left for us to execute at that level.

And yet, the job wasn't done. To complete the mission of creating a sustainable culture of change, the unit of change had to shift to the ultimate goal of our mission: user satisfaction with every IBM product and service.

It was evident almost immediately that the universal experiences had brought forth a newfound alignment between top-level priorities and team-level execution. Essentially, we provided IBM with a shared language for targeting and scaling impactful outcomes. By introducing the specific terminologies of the nine user contexts, we clarified where specific teams were underperforming in ways that everyone on the organization chart could understand, discuss, and take action on. This enabled us to transform even the most entrenched shared services by making their specific contribution to product success visible, measurable, and accountable.

Although speed is always invoked as the number one concern of corporate senior leadership, it's rarely acknowledged that the chief impediment to moving faster is the absence of a shared language that is concrete enough to pierce through bias and bluster. At IBM, design thinking and Agile was at the root of this shared language, but even though our CMO, CIO, and other centralized functions had taken up the new way of work, sharing the same toolsets and tool chains, that still wasn't enough to align everyone on the outcomes we aimed to provide.

But now, with the universal experiences embedded in a governance structure for measuring and monitoring, IBM's shared language could be deployed to drive alignment on which experience(s) to prioritize, across all those silos. Understanding exactly which context a particular offering was deficient in drove faster decision-making about specifically what to do next, and clear-cut actions that needed to be taken even across disparate silos and shared services. Without metrics at this level of granularity, executives are driven to make simple and fast judgments that are often wrong, or they get mired in the back and forth of what ifs that bog down decision-making processes.

When people ask me how to transform massive shared services legacy functions, I tell them to stop trying to change the entire organization at once. Instead, determine where it's affecting only your most important product or service's users and surgically transform that touchpoint first. With the credibility gained through visible wins, let the success create demand for broader change. That's how even the most resistant parts of IBM came to embrace our mission of change. Everyone wants better. Show it to them. Give to them. They'll always want more.

So, How Do You Know You're Finished?

I believe you are finished when you can measure and change your end user's end-to-end experiences, across all their touchpoints, with confidence that your new change provocation is contributing to each result. What had once constituted change now constitutes the status quo. The priorities of the business, not the change team, are now driving adoption.

This doesn't mean everything and everyone has been changed, and it doesn't mean that what's changed is perfect. What it means is that the organization is able to see the through lines of the new skills, practices, processes and systems in the work of *every team touching those outcomes*. This is as true for AI as it is for design.

Until you're able to do that, across the spectrum of product, sales, marketing, legal, and all the rest, then you'll never know if an outcome truly reveals the change effort. You can make tweaks, for example, change the product team and improve the product, but if marketing, support, and sales are not on the same page, it's hard to make sense of your outcomes. If the old culture still exists in a crucial department like sales, they may thwart everything that's been done by the product team.

That's where we were when we started with the very first Hallmark team. We didn't have the benefit of the universal experiences as a guiding light. We were measuring metrics based on team behaviors: ramping up teams, looking at their artifacts, listening to their playbacks. Of course, this is all you can do day one. You can't change everything at once. But over time, as the sales of IBM products continued to underperform, even when the NPS data told us the user experience was much better, it would have been easy to conclude that the new way of working wasn't the right remedy after all. In fact, all it meant was that we were still far from finishing the job.

Final Day

In January 2020, when IBM had its annual kickoff meeting in New York with the top 300 executives in the organization, it was announced that Ginni Rometty would be retiring as CEO in April. Her successor would be Arvind Krishna, the IBM senior vice president whom I had reported to since 2018, when Robert LeBlanc retired.

With Robert and Ginni both gone, I would be the only key player left from the change program that we had started in 2012. By now, the Hallmark name had been retired, and the office I headed was no longer a change program in any meaningful sense. It was a small, central design office responsible for owning IBMs design language and maintaining what was now a vast, distributed community of designers (3,000 and counting, at the time). As a design program, it needed a designer in charge. It was time for me to move on.

By the time of Arvind's announcement as CEO January 2020, I'd already advised him that I planned to retire by June 2021 and that I would hire my successor before that. Following the IBM kickoff, I planned to spend half of 2020 traveling outside the country, where I'd be doing client work while also visiting IBM Studios around the world for one last time. At home in Austin, my wife and I decided that with me on the road so often, it would be an ideal time to do a renovation of our house. We moved to a small apartment while demolition started on the house in December 2019. I'd be home on weekends, and it would be cozy and fun.

I was in Zurich in late February 2020 when COVID-19 had already begun to ravage Italy. I flew to a meeting in Los Angeles before returning home, just as the world shut down. Arvind asked me to stay on extra year or two, and I accepted. No one knew how long the pandemic would last and I understood why he didn't want to add design to the many things he had to worry about.

My focus for the crisis year of 2020 shifted away from travel and toward the task of keeping IBM's design thinking community intact and productive. The work we had done with our places paid off, because we already had a playbook for how to make the most of remote interaction. Yes, work is better in person, but we also knew how to have productive collaborations on distributed teams with, for example, engineering in Germany, development in Hyderabad, and design in Prague.

As I made preparations to leave by June 2022, I was mindful of something I'd said from the very early days: that the true test of whether something is sustainable is to see what happens when the founder or first leader exits. That's always the big question when a startup prepares to be bought out. Are the systems and processes strong enough to survive the change in leadership?

What I discovered is that by scaling change and making it stick, I had solved this question for myself. Every element of culture change I'd been hired to implement in 2012 had been systematically scaled up and transferred into IBM's business units by 2022. Design thinking, Agile, new HR designations, all the new tools—these were all just part of the new normal. The changes we'd hoped would go viral when we started had fully infected IBM's host body. All the teamwork functions that originated with Hallmark were now operating not as exciting exemplars of change but as emblems of IBM's new status quo.

During my time at IBM, we saw powerful signals that these and other cultural changes were taking root—employee engagement climbing by 30 to 40 percent, clients expressing renewed enthusiasm for working with us, and teams spontaneously adopting new ways of working. Yet the revenue growth that would validate these changes in the financial markets remained elusive.

This is one of the humbling realities of leading transformation at scale. The most meaningful business outcomes emerging from change will arise long after the initial work is done. Transformation creates waves that ripple far beyond the coming fiscal year. The work we did—changing how people collaborate, how teams form, how spaces function—was all the essential groundwork for a future yet to be even dreamed of. To borrow from an old proverb, the job of change agents is to plant seedlings for trees whose shade we know we will never sit under.

A CEO I respect once shared this perspective that's stayed with me ever since: "Never judge a CEO by what happened on their watch; evaluate the CEO by what happens on the next CEO's watch." There's profound wisdom in recognizing that our most important contributions might be invisible during our tenure.

IBM's path in subsequent years suggests that the cultural changes we initiated in the previous decade have contributed to IBM's recent successes. I make no claim to that credit—too many talented leaders and teams have worked tirelessly in the years since to build on the foundation we helped construct.

Perhaps the most valuable lesson is simply this: meaningful change requires patience and humility. The leader's job isn't to ensure they're present for the victory lap. Rather, it is to do the quiet, foundational work that makes future success possible, regardless of who receives the accolades. The beauty of irresistible change is that it no longer needed me—the design for change that we built will continue evolving, the incentives we put in place have enduring momentum, and we made the experience so enticing that our people couldn't resist more.

On my final day at IBM, I attended one last Campfire at the Austin studio. I told everyone there that I loved them, and how proud I was to have joined them on this journey into the unknown. I called Katrina Alcorn, IBM's new head of design, to say goodbye and wish her well. Then I headed out of the Austin studio and into the elevator for the last time. There was nothing left to do at IBM for a product guy whose product for nine years had been irresistible change.

Takeaways

- **The name goes away:** At some point, the changes will have been so broadly adopted that the brand name goes away, with the values and practices underpinning the brand fully integrated into the organization's everyday way of work. All project teams are expected to have adopted the new ways, to one degree or another. However, this still may not be the end.
- **End-to-end accountability:** To ensure change is fully adopted, you should instantiate a measurement system, like NPS or whatever measures the outcome you seek, that monitors the quality of the outcomes you seek across every touchpoint. Ownership of this system and responses to deficiencies are in the C-suite. Business outcomes drive activities, not team behaviors. This is the end game.
- **The new status quo:** Everything possible is embedded in the decentralized business. The program office is downsized and shifts to being a center of competency for the *change provocation*, but only those aspects that make sense to be shared. Systems and processes have been changed and are in place to reinforce the new culture. What was new is old again.

Appendix:
The Irresistible
Experiences Playbook

With every passing year of IBM's cultural transformation, I grew more convinced that the design of a change program at its start is absolutely critical to its outcomes. Key choices we made early on continued to have a profound effect on the results we achieved through year four and beyond. And so many times along the way—as we evolved our business development system, our management system, our certification programs to instill and nurture Coaches and Advocates—I wished we had known to do these kinds of things much sooner than we did.

If your organization is delivering lackluster outcomes or, perhaps, wanting your people back in the office; or maybe it's a reorganization or the need to embrace the power of a new technology like artificial intelligence (AI), how do you start? I'd recommend you pick up where the IBM transformation left off, by designing your program to elegantly address each of the touchpoints described by the universal experiences, described in Chapter 10.

Begin with the understanding that you are selling the ultimate luxury good. Sustainable cultural change, like any other product in the luxury category, is rare, highly desirable, and above all, it deeply engages the emotions. Change is both difficult and powerful because it challenges people's prior beliefs and assumptions about what is possible in their careers and their lives. I could have filled another book with the testimonials of countless IBMers whose careers blossomed and took off under our new way of work. Many had never imagined that a career with IBM could be so exciting, that it would stretch their capabilities and offer them so many opportunities for advancement. The change product you offer will transform people's lives for the better in ways that can't be counted.

When conceiving the specific experiences your program will deliver, keep in mind that all of these contexts are transitory, so a key objective within each of the nine universal experiences is to ease the handoff from one user state to another (from *Discover* to *Learn*, for example, or from *Try* to *Get help*). Meanwhile, you must be mindful of your capabilities at each stage. Be careful about putting time and resources into helping employees discover and learn if you don't have some answer for them when they want to try it out. That's one thing I knew from decades as a product guy. Do not raise expectations beyond what your offering is ready to provide *now*. In Chapter 1 I told of how a perfectly prepared cupcake is more satisfying than a half-baked wedding cake. This is what I meant. Once you've gained your customers' precious attention, they will want the chance to try and buy. Responding to that desire promptly, even if you can't provide the full-blown wedding cake experience, is essential to success in today's consumer culture.

Which raises an important point: the people who participate in your change program are your customers, and you must always treat them as such. This is especially important among your early adopters. If they don't stick with your program, you must assume it's your fault and seek ways to fix what's not working. Even the people at the other end of the spectrum, who are resisting the very idea of change, represent a customer service failure on your part. Why? Because no one hates improvement. Everyone who resists change perceives it as some kind of threat—to their career, their status or their authority. And at first glance the nature of that perceived threat may not seem obvious to you.

It takes a disciplined customer service mentality to learn about these threats and address them. You need to know your customers well enough to understand how to help them with their problems. Some of these problems may seem trivial to you, but they are as serious as your customer says they are. If you treat your customers with respect and take even their silliest-sounding concerns seriously, you will come up with no end of creative solutions to the problems at hand. That's what we found, time and time again. Resistance and obstacles led us to one breakthrough solution after another because we never gave in to the idea that "they just don't get it."

The Personas of Change

In this model, every change program has a customer base represented by personas designed to address the needs of three critical stakeholders: senior executives, middle managers (which I call *line executives*), and team members. Each of these three groups experience your change product very differently, and every detail of every experience you offer them must be tailored to address their distinct concerns.

Depending on your organization's size, I would define the senior executives as those people who are one or two levels under the most senior sponsoring officer. In the case of IBM, the CEO was the sponsoring officer, and the senior executives included both her directs, the senior vice presidents (SVPs) who ran entire business units, and their directs, the general managers (GMs) in charge of IBM's various lines of business. Every senior executive is different, but there are some commonalities you can count on, including that they know that change is needed. Their chief concern, I've found, is that change will either take too long or it will fail to scale. Because they are several levels above the project teams doing the actual work, the change program is a unique opportunity to bring them in closer touch with how work is actually getting done. That connection, through the common language of the universal experiences, proved to be a transformative achievement at IBM. You can start building that common language on day one.

The unique problems of the line executive tend to be overlooked in change programs. These critical people are either ignored completely (which was my mistake) or they are treated like a team member and educated in the change provocation when what they need is an understanding of how to manage a team that is adopting the change provocation. Although every executive will ultimately fall into this category, the line executive *experience* applies only to those who are in the line between a team in the program and the senior sponsoring officer. Remember, only work with teams—and their line executives—who are admitted into the program, in their real-world work context. During the change program, these people must run their upline organization in the old culture even as they manage a mix of teams under them working in new and radically different ways. Interestingly, line executives sometimes don't see the need for change as critically as those at the top and the bottom of the org chart. It's perhaps more accurate to say that they don't see the need for *their* operations to be upended by change. Addressing the rationale for change and how it would affect them through a special training and certification as Advocates proved to be very helpful in our cultivation of middle management support.

As with the senior executive, every team member also knows that change is necessary, but for different reasons. Team members are always affected the most by old-fashioned work habits and inefficient operations—which cause the need for most transformation efforts. What they fear about transformation is that either the changes won't be radical enough to have impact or that the organization won't have the fortitude to see things through. They also may have some trepidation that a failing change program will tar their careers. Your change program will stand out in the eyes of a team member if it provides continuing evidence that the changes are working and spreading. These are the people you'll get to know the best and spend the most time with, and their outcomes will reflect directly on your program's early success.

For the rest of the book, I'll describe how the irresistible change model is intended to work for each of these stakeholder groups (senior executives, line executives, and team members) across all of the model's touchpoints. My hope is that the recommendations and examples I offer will spur some useful idea generation among you and your team. Many of the items discussed seem very simple in nature, but delivering these experiences across the board with consistent excellence requires discipline and intentionality. Your odds of success increase with every successful touchpoint, and you'll seldom go wrong if you keep reminding yourself that you are in the hospitality business. As I told my staff before our first bootcamp, we weren't doing these teams a favor—they were doing us a favor. They were giving us their time and trusting us not to abuse it. The people who come to you do so with open hearts. It's your job to turn them into loving hearts, becoming fellow travelers on the journey of irresistible change (Figure A.1).

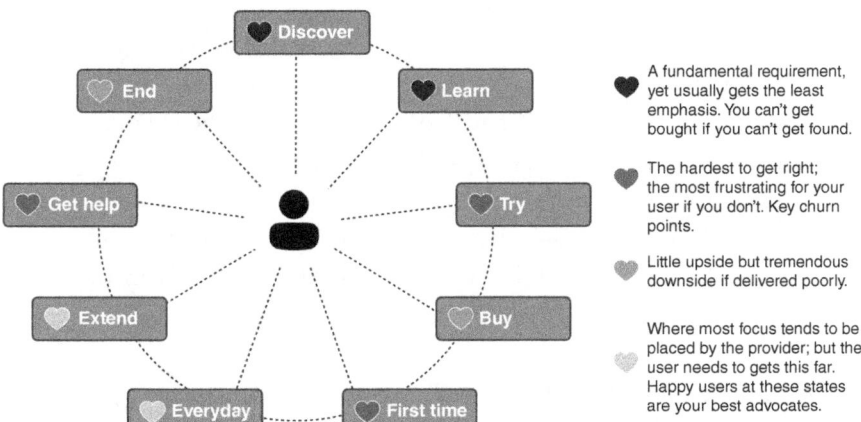

Figure A.1   Nine universal contexts in which users experience a product or service.

Discover

I'm pretty aware of what's going on, and I'm constantly on the lookout for new solutions. Why haven't I heard of you?

Seems pretty obvious: you won't be considered if you can't be found. You'd be surprised how many products don't focus on being found. For example, this isn't simply about showing up in search results, although that's one way to be found. It's not about waiting for your user to find you, it's about finding them, and introducing yourself. You need to know *where* your users are, not just *who* they are, and meet them there.

- **Senior executive:** Before your initial teams get started, this is the key audience you need to be discovered by, and possibly the only one. Fortunately, the fact that a change program exists is probably the result of senior leadership establishing it. So something about the effort will be known and, generally, the senior folks already accept the need for change. What they need next is to believe in the solution you propose, your capabilities as the leader and your plan for scaling. They will also want to know that you've studied and learned from the examples of other companies that have pursued this change and benefited. In addition to communicating this information, this is also your chance to make a sales pitch for soliciting teams to enroll in the program.
- **Line executive:** These overlooked middle managers need special attention. This was one of the hardest audiences to develop a *Discover* experience for. They aren't hearing about your program from their leadership in the same way senior executives are hearing from, say, the CEO. It's not uncommon for senior leadership to have spent quarters on the program, and line executives to hear about it only weeks or days before it's being implemented. You should work to change this, making them feel more included as early as possible, without overloading them with details that they, specifically, may be months or years from having to futz with. At IBM, I met them at technical summits, town halls, and through site visits where local leadership would assemble all site executives. As soon as you have results to show, see if you can get those results in front of the line executives in a way that enhances your credibility. In Hallmark's case

we were fortunate to be invited by Ginni's team to give a presentation at the CEO's January 2014 kickoff with IBM's top 300 global executives in attendance. Because it came at the start of our year two, after our initial cohort of projects had been launched, we were able to offer real-world stories of change instead of speculative evangelistic claptrap. In terms of discovering us, that visibility turned out to be worth its weight in gold.

- **Team member:** Your team members want to see themselves in the change. For all personas, but especially for team members, nothing sells change more effectively than showing happy colleagues who've blazed the trail ahead of them. At Hallmark we filled the company intranet with videos of real IBMers expressing delight at their bootcamp experience—peers showing how work changed for the better. Later, we'd use external trade press and analysts to tell our story publicly, knowing that these reports would reflect back and cause chatter inside the company. That one *New York Times* Sunday Business section cover article in 2014 probably generated as much internal discovery among team members and line executives than all the other things we'd done combined! In today's media environment, you must find out where your people are and introduce yourself there. Like any other direct-to-consumer business, you want to encourage satisfied customers to share their personal stories on social media, blog sites, bulletin boards. Use every available channel to enhance your *Discover* experience. In Hallmark's case, we even bought a printing press!

Learn

What is this, and why do you think it solves my problem?.

People learn in so many different ways that you must be prepared to deliver material about your program and its provocation across a broad range of media. Some car buyers will read dozens of automotive reviews before choosing one dealer showroom to visit. Others will make the rounds of dealerships and do a half-dozen test drives instead. Buyers like these, who skip right to the try experience, are people who like to merge the learn and try experiences. Trying something is their preferred way to learn about it. As best as you can, offer some portion of *Try* in your *Learn* experience and *Learn* in your *Try* experience, so that you can capture all types of buyers.

- **Senior executive:** Your first slide decks shown to senior executives should be the one area where exercising a little future-forecasting evangelization is helpful. You must demonstrate the value of your approach to the new thing in terms that respond to their big concerns: impact, speed, and scale. Your learning materials should quell their skepticism that change is doable in a timely manner and can be affordably scaled, while also being realistic. Our quarterly calls with senior executives were crucial learning experiences that we delivered. These calls, quarter after quarter, year after year, created a common language for team health and new skills that proved transformative at IBM.

- **Line executive:** If I had to do it all over again, we would have offered our line executives a primer on what Hallmark teams are and how to manage them side by side with all their other teams doing things the old way. All we could have offered at first would have been our informed hypotheses, but we would have drafted the document or course with the advice of one or more sympathetic line executives. That would have been an invaluable learning experience for *us*, to hear in advance how our program was likely to affect the daily lives of IBM's line executives. The initial *Learn* experience you prepare for this audience will ultimately provide the basic material for what later might be a scalable executive learning experience similar to the IBM Advocate training and certification.

- **Team member:** Some people will want to learn everything there is to know about your plans before the program even starts, and you have to be ready for that. In the preparation phase before the program launches, consider how blogs and other simple forms of communication can communicate how you will be approaching change. In our case, I went a little overboard. I personally wrote up a detailed 30-page document titled "IBM Design Thinking" and distributed it as a PDF file to anyone who asked. My intention was to lay out the mechanics of our approach and, just as importantly, describe the new cultural values we were seeking. The document had enough depth to assure our earliest supporters that our initiative was authentically dedicated to shift IBM culture in ways that mattered. These details helped ensure skeptics would feel that the coming change would be substantive, and not mere performative window dressing. Later we developed a fairly comprehensive website with all manner of content and resources to satisfy the curiosity of people interested in learning more about Hallmark and the new people, practices, and places of IBM.

Try

Sounds interesting. I'd like to play with it to see if it's as good as you say, and preferably without you hovering over me. Why do you need to know my name?

Together with *First time use*, I consider *Try* one of the most important experiences on the path to adoption. *Try* is a high-stakes matter for you, the seller. If your users don't enjoy trying, they're not going to be buying! The best *Try* experience is always one that is show, not tell.

For digital product sales, these experiences often enable prospects to sample a digital tool using simulated data in a safe, sandboxed environment. Change programs, however, are service offerings that can't similarly offer fake access to the expertise. Providing a *Try* experience, then, is more about offering a zero-risk experience for the first-time buyer. Opt-in-only was always our number one principle, accompanied by the guarantee of a no-judgment opt-out at any point.

Your users will always compare your change product to the status quo, which is your competition. Keep in mind that the most memorable experiences not only have measurable impact but also stir the soul.

- **Senior executive:** After learning about the program, the senior executive needs to commit one or two teams to it, from the dozens or hundreds under their command. There is cost and there is risk, but it is limited. The *Try* experience should provide complete transparency so that if they feel like something is going off the rails, they have the ability to correct it or even pull their team out of the program. All this needs to be communicated up front, as a part of a great *Try* experience. "We'd like to work with one or two of your teams to figure out how change will work best in your world. If we're successful, we have a plan for scaling the program quickly after that." This audience's desired outcome of *Try* is to understand three things: their employees' perceptions of the change, the timeliness of getting their project to market, and the market outcome.

- **Line executive:** Much like the senior executive, the line executive should understand the ease with which their team or teams can try the new approach. You will also be working with the line executive in a set of trial-focused meetings to help them understand how the changes will affect them as managers. In those instances, even the lightest weight Advocate-style training could help provide all line executives (up to the most senior executive) with some useful advice about how to work with their trial team. Consider adding line executives alongside the team members for key parts of their team's training sessions in your new way of working. We never did that with our bootcamps, and that oversight was a series of missed opportunities.

- **Team member:** In the early days, I strongly advise designing *Try* experiences that are as real-world, hands-on, and analog as possible. That's more expensive than digital training, I know, but at the start I believe it's worth it. Our bootcamps for our first seven teams constituted our biggest investment, both in the program resources we dedicated to putting them on and because we paid for the teams' travel, hotels, and other logistics. Team members invested their time away from home, but otherwise, we delivered the entire week as though it were a "freemium" offer, and it worked. Teams eventually started gladly paying to experience what we'd given the first seven teams for free. As people outside the program office gained expertise in our new ways, we were able to move our *Try* experience to a free online course (and Practitioner badge). Later, earning this badge would become a prerequisite to attending a (shortened) bootcamp. Eventually, the bootcamps themselves were no longer necessary.

Buy

Love it. But you don't take Apple Pay? Ugh.

Don't make it difficult to buy your thing! That's easy to say but difficult to perfect. Is the pricing clear and fair for everyone? Is the transaction itself painless? How do you negotiate discounts for those who ask?

In our case, when we started charging our teams for participation, we suddenly had to deal with the labyrinth that is big company procurement! What this meant in practical terms is that we as the seller tried to take the multiple pains of this process off our buyers' shoulders and put that pain squarely on our own. We didn't enjoy it, but it was necessary. We couldn't afford the risk of having buyers quit on us simply because they felt thwarted by the procurement process.

- **Senior executive:** We relentlessly gave these folks forward visibility into financial road maps for their teams' participation in Hallmark, including bootcamp costs and any new head count. We'd always start these financial conversations at the GM level, then roll up to the aggregate SVP level across their multiple GMs. Then we'd work directly with their chief financial officer (CFO), ensuring that the road maps agreed with the SVP made it into the fall plan and other budgeting and expense processes. This was a critical function of my team; without it, we would have, at best, significantly lengthened the time the program took to succeed.
- **Line executive:** We kept line executives informed throughout the buying process, especially with respect to the tactical release of funds required of specific teams. Of course, they were privy to all the road maps negotiated with the senior executives they reported to and, often, would contribute support in their own business unit meetings.
- **Team member:** At the team level, people weren't typically savvy about what was required to get the budget from the CFO, especially the major processes of the fall plan. And even beyond the fall plan

budget, the team leaders typically didn't have the power (or confidence) to get funds released if there was any friction at all. So, my team developed deep relationships across all CFO offices. Once we had SVP approval, we would engage on behalf of each team to get their desired allocation. Where there was a mismatch between an SVP and their CFO, we would work to resolve it. Tactically, those same relationships enabled us to engage directly on behalf of each team to then get those funds released, solving problems they didn't even know they had.

First Time Use

Here's my real information and first problem; can you help me solve it? I appreciate the hand-holding while I ramp up on this; it's right there where I want it, when I need it.

Of the nine experiences, I have studied this one the most extensively because there is ample evidence of its primary importance. Research has shown that a customer's satisfaction with the value gained from their first use of a product is highly predictive of whether they will become a regular user. In this model, the success of the whole change program rests on whether the first week bootcamp persuades the teams to adopt the new way of working.

Some people might imagine that, for example, a software wizard, or pointing at or talking about new features, is a good *First time use* experience. It's not. It isn't good for your user unless some real personal or business value has been achieved. Delivering a good *First time use* experience is somewhat like giving a new bike rider a soft surface to ride on with you running alongside, keeping the rider from falling. Giving them the thrill of pedaling themselves and going faster than they've ever gone before. They're hooked! The controlled conditions you give them reduces their risk which speeds up their willingness to try, so they can more quickly feel their exhilaration from doing the new thing. It's not a simulation or a video presentation. It's the real-world thing with enhanced support.

There may be elements of learning and trying embedded in *First time use*, but this is what makes it a distinct experience: the user is actually doing the thing, developing personal capabilities in the new thing and deriving value from it. That's where your focus should be in designing *First time use* experiences.

- **Senior executive:** For these busy folks, the experience began with our first meeting after a team had started in Hallmark. We prepared thoroughly, showing up five minutes early but prepared to finish in 15 minutes or less, even if scheduled for 30. I wanted our call to be the one that got them back on schedule, a small but meaningful courtesy. This introduced to them a structure and language that signaled "this is different from your other meetings." Whatever that difference might be; in our case, it was a perfectly designed pitch deck that provoked conversation about the topics of change, as opposed to the typical reporting tools and verbose slide deck.

- **Line executive:** In the same way the team members engage during the bootcamp, the line executives for a given Hallmark team should show up (virtually or in person) for a couple of times during the bootcamp. They'll begin to connect the dots between the artifacts and language of the team, and those that they'll be using upstream. While there will be many line executives for a given team, one or two will suffice to be named as primary. There should be some programmatic interaction with them post-bootcamp to see how they're perceiving their team, in the new world. Using the new language that the change program has introduced, help them translate all this into their upline reporting needs.

- **Team member:** Our bootcamp was designed around the premise that the team would realize shocking breakthroughs by Friday morning's wrap-up (playback). Even when teams started paying for Hallmark, we always made this offer: If doing this work for five days hasn't benefited your team, you're free to leave. No team ever did, but that freedom was essential to giving teams the autonomy people crave when doing unfamiliar things. My team handled 100 percent of the logistics, from airfare to hotel, and every day's inside and outside programming (we let people do their own thing Wednesday and Thursday nights). When I say every aspect, I mean it. We had hotel blocks reserved every week so that the new teams would be together—often collaborating in the hallways. We had transportation lined up every morning and evening. Aside from the in-bootcamp experience, which was first rate, every part of the that week sent the message: this is different. This is special.

Everyday Use

Look, ma, no hands! I can use this every day or once a year, and I always feel comfortable and in control.

Designing for the *Everyday use* experience means preparing not only the team to adopt new ways of working but also the people, systems, and processes around them to facilitate full-time adoption. The training wheels are off, and your change offering integrates easily into the user's everyday reality. A great *Everyday use* experience assumes that users are smart and resourceful enough to personalize the product to better fit their needs. Think about where people and when people will be using your product and then cater the design to their behaviors and other tools they're using. This is one reason I didn't get overly dogmatic on, for example, the specific practices of design thinking or Agile.

The fundamental experiences underpinning *Try*, *First time use*, and *Everyday use* should be the same, like the car you test drive is fundamentally the same as the one you buy. But it can still be an enormous leap to use something in the real world, every day, without guardrails. This is why designing and delivering the *Everyday use* experience is so difficult, especially in a services-based offering like change. It's a critical point of potential failure because there are so many real-world constraints that will affect adoption of any new change provocation.

Sending the bootcampers out of that controlled environment and back into their everyday world had us on pins and needles. It was one of the highest-risk thresholds we faced.

- ■ **Senior executive:** For these folks, *Everyday use* was mainly designed around the quarterly meetings and evolving the management deck into something that meaningfully affected more of their life. First it was just informational, then it moved into something that drove head count and budgets. And finally it would prove to be a tool that drove outcomes and reflected the new capabilities in their business. We evolved these touchpoints based on what we learned, just like any startup would improve its product over time. These executives' needs will shift over time, primarily driven by the materiality of their financial investment, measured by the number and importance of the teams in the program.

- **Line executive:** Line executives needed to be able to easily context switch between their old teams and their new teams. This came easier for some than others. Our psychiatrists were primarily supporting the team members but also spent a fair amount of time in what was effectively our *Everyday use* experience for line executives. Once we'd come to understand them and created the Advocate program, their days got easier and they grew more engaged. At the beginning, we had to learn about their world in order for us to modify our product, and offer a quality *Everyday use* experience for them. For example, the program team eased the everyday lives of line executives by bringing IBM's systems into alignment with the new way of working, from new tooling access to updated career ladders.

- **Team member:** Be humble in the early days of change. Don't assume you know exactly how the offering will work for your first-time users once they return to the real world. We knew our boot-camp was a good *First time use* experience, but everything they needed were tuned for the week's activities. For example, during bootcamp our product teams weren't interfacing with their real source control systems. But when they returned from bootcamp, they would be. How would that go? We had no idea, but knew that all the marbles were on the table. Our best risk-reduction measure was sending out on-site support in the form of our psychiatrists. Their purpose was twofold. First, they helped teams integrate the new way of working into their everyday world, but more importantly they reported back to us on the specific problems the teams were facing *so that we could find solutions.* We quickly discovered the inadequacy of IBM's tooling and the need for teams to upgrade to new products like Slack, Github, and Mural. By the end of year two, the need for psychiatrists was greatly reduced because most of the common obstacles to everyday use had been encountered and overcome. Even then we continued to probe, leading to our discovery of the shit umbrellas and the magic people. As with any startup, our user experience kept improving through a relentless focus on how our users were faring.

Extend

All these add-ons and additional use cases I can bring to this are awesome, and I can scale easily because others are also using this.

The goal of the change program is to lay the foundation for sustained adoption of the new way of working, not simply to insert a new skill here and there. Your program's success will bring with it highly engaged users eager to participate more broadly in establishing the new culture. You owe it to them and to your program to prepare new experiences in response to the demand you've created.

Think of this like photo sharing with your family. Using a smartphone's camera and photo storage is great, but leveraging those same skills and easily sharing those photos with friends in the same device ecosystem creates stickiness that's harder to overcome. Figuring out where extensions like this can increase the value your users get from your new ways of work will reinforce the change provocation in ways beyond just its tactical use on a project team.

- **Senior executive:** Senior executives participate by expanding their commitment to the program. Prepare for all the natural concerns aroused by the expansion of teams. Ease the way by addressing budgetary concerns, new skills required in their organization, and ensuring the right expertise is available for responsible expansion. In the case of IBM, we needed to help senior leadership to respond to rapidly changing priorities by helping them continuously adjust their investments in change and the project teams. We used the *Everyday use* experience to tee up conversations about extending the program more deeply into their areas of the business. This didn't happen by chance, but by designing exactly how we wanted the *Extend* experience to happen, from the time frame it occurred over to the cost and funding of it.

- **Line executive:** Same with the line executive. Be ready to expand visibility into these executives' multiple teams' behaviors, road maps, and project progress. The easier you make it for them to provide reports upward, the better. Operational insights into teams are typically new details that no management systems have; create a scalable way to share this with them when, say, a line executive has more than two teams in the program.

- **Team member:** It's a nice thing to have people step forward because they are turned on to change. Try not to let them down. You want everyone in the organization to have a personal stake in the change initiative, and the best way to do that is to make change a pathway to opportunity. We designed for an individual's *Extend* experience like this: how can we provide future career paths that would both increase the individual's options for the future (career pathing), while also securing more and more power for the program's goals to be sustained (executive roles). See to it that human resources (HR) systems are updated for virtually every type of person in the organization so that aptitude in the new way of working is included in the standards by which promotions and raises are judged.

And beyond that, people who say they want to expand their involvement in change are telling you that their hearts have been touched by the possibilities. The mindset of people in this phase is one of hope, trust, and excitement. While everyone was expected to have the beginner's Practitioner badge, becoming a Co-creator or Coach was perhaps the first and most highly scalable way we offered team members to participate more broadly in the culture shift. For many team member superfans, we also offered one-year rotations on the Hallmark program team, which was not only a fun diversion from their typical work but it also gave them a glimpse into leadership and working at enterprise scale at earlier points in their career than normal.

Get Help

I'm stuck. What do I do next?

From the start of the program, if you can embrace the values of hospitality and transparency, your customers will feel assured that you are truly available to help them through any situation, from *Discover* to *End use*. Therefore, *Get help* is a very important experience to get right. It's one of my three "code red" experiences, along with *Try* and *First time use*. If you get it wrong, you suffer inordinate damage to your brand and product reputation from which you may not recover. And because, unlike those two, which are only temporary contexts (you can't be trying or using something for the first time forever), obtaining help is always required. This is the one context that is delivered in relation to every other context, save *Discover*. It is also the one most likely operating on a shoestring budget! It doesn't have to be expensive, but it has to be delivered with care.

- **Senior executive:** Taking the burden of the CFO-related work off the plate of the senior executive was a big one. The senior executive obviously was in the approval loop, but the detailed spreadsheets and what have you were taken care of between my team and the CFO. Embedding a senior leader with responsibility for the change agenda was also an aspect of making access to help about the program easier and faster. Of course, we were also *always* on call available to any of these people. Over all the years, I doubt if there was ever a communication that went unanswered within 30 minutes to an hour to this group.
- **Line executive:** The Advocate program created a network where middle managers could connect and share challenges. We supplemented this with our broader community efforts and maintained our friendly policy that anyone could just call us directly. No barriers, no gatekeepers. In addition, in time we would add new executives into the business units directly responsible for design, design thinking, and related Agile practices. Because of their organizational proximity, these peers would be the first people a Hallmark team's line executive would typically contact. They would know the business unit's

context much better than we would and proved pivotal to providing real-time assistance when issues arose.

- **Team member:** The most important helpers with the initial teams were the psychiatrists who observed and reported back to us in the program office. Later as we developed our Coach community, that network provided invaluable help. Going forward, this is a community I'd identify and nurture from day one. We kept the technical bar for asking for help low (primarily Slack) and ensured community managers kept questions from languishing. Nothing damages the reputation of a premium brand with more certainty than unanswered calls for help. Generally speaking, if I heard of someone not being answered within one day I was on my team's case about it.

End Use

What happens when I'm finished using your product?

Understanding *End use* is not something to be put off. Here, when I'm talking about *End use*, I'm not referring to the team but to the program. Thoughtfully considered, it will inform a significant part of the to-be vision of your change program. All of your stakeholders will want to know what success looks like, as the program office transfers its critical functions gradually into the business. This will look a little different for every change program, depending on the nature of your change provocation, but the principle is the same in this model. The branded product will go away and the program office should be designed to dissolve.

When change has gone viral and the host body has been figuratively fully infected with the new way of working, the change program no longer needs to function as protector of a fragile new thing. With critical skeptics vanquished, the systems upgraded, and adoption throughout the supply chain of outcomes, the new thing has transformed into the status quo. At that point, all that should remain of the change program office is something that looks like a center of competency to support and maintain shared parts of the original change provocation. Mind you, the broader culture may not be the utopia of change you envisioned, but that is not the same as rejecting the change. As the leader, you have to accept that, like the fusing of genes, the new plus old is now a hybrid culture that will maintain itself *in whatever fashion it chooses.*

- **Senior executive:** Be sure you start by giving the top a picture of what to expect when change takes place at scale. There should be a vision of how the transfer of responsibilities should be handled, and what the final structure of the change program is destined to look like, including a provisional to-be org chart. Some corporate executive (in our case it was the CMO) should be anticipated as the appropriate authority for evaluating external outcomes delivered in the new ways. In our case, the transfer meant establishing a new team, outside the Hallmark umbrella, that was chaired by the CMO. I attended as simply an involved executive. This provided continuity while also signaling the shift in responsibility. For measurement, we used net promoter score (NPS) to monitor user experiences. For a corporate AI implementation, it might be similar NPS monitoring but targeted specifically at AI touchpoints to detect where AI might be struggling to improve business outcomes.

- **Line executive:** Program *End use* for the line executive is basically the transition point when the majority of business operations of their teams has shifted from the old to the new, and there's a peer inside the same organizational unit who owns the provocation and the outcomes it's designed to affect. At that point, there's very little emphasis on program resources (like Hallmark, in my case). As you design this experience, consider how your line executives' operating worlds have changed after all their teams are operating in this new way. How are the reports, systems, and processes around them changed so that they reinforce the line executive's continued new behaviors?

- **Team member:** Hopefully a team and its members will never end their use of the tools. Like Netflix, the goal is for them to become lifelong subscribers. But with respect to the program, there is a point for every team and individual when their relationship to the program ends, and their interaction with everyday systems and processes provides all the reinforcement they need.

Initially, we built into their bootcamp experience transparency into the *End use* decision ("you can leave here on Friday and never hear from us again"). This gave them agency and helped them get past the "mandate" obstacle most change programs suffer from.

As the practices matured and the results came in, it was clear that this new thing was good, and the culture embraced it. It defined who we were, as IBM. At that point, the systems and processes of the embedded culture start working in your favor. Working in these new ways became an expected aspect of everyone's job, and this was encoded into the job descriptions of our HR career ladders. It was all still opt-in or opt-out; the decision was yours, and the consequences of non-participation were easy to understand. *End use* doesn't always end as happily as canceling Netflix, but you can still make it easy and clear.

And Again?

The new status quo deserves your disdain…

To be a change agent is to always be questioning the status quo. After your new culture sticks, it's only a matter of time before it starts to calcify. Trust and transparency may decline, and systems may get bogged down by fanatical rules following (for example, rituals for design thinking and Agile are as prone to becoming performative as anything else). Your new normal will always be better than your old normal, but the need for yet another round of change is never far off, driven by the next disruptive technology or new methodology. Be watchful. The organizations destined to thrive in this century will be those that develop an irresistible appetite for change.

Acknowledgments

Two years after I left IBM, I was at a client's leadership team off-site in Zurich. After I finished my bit the CEO told me the next item on the agenda was a presentation of some AI work they'd done with IBM. Would I care to stick around and watch?

The joint IBM and client team had no idea who I was as they started going over the status of the six projects they were collaborating on. They spoke of running design sprints and working in IBM Garages. They showed their user research, their journey maps, and the wire frames they were designing in response to the various insights. Nobody thought anything unusual about it. To all of them—the client's team, the IBMers, the client's top executives—this was simply how IBM works. They had no idea what it had taken to make that happen. I didn't say anything, but I was so proud and even a bit emotional inside.

Ruminating on the trip home, I found it was a very humbling experience, because I had nothing to do with so much of what has been accomplished. Thousands of people worked harder than me to fulfill my promises to Ginni and Robert. The whole thing had been at times so close to not happening at all. There were other candidates for the job of leading change at IBM, but it was Robert who had said, "No, Phil's the guy." That was a big gamble on his part. What I was proposing was not how change is usually introduced. And if he had made the wrong bet on the wrong person, it could have really blown up in his face. He's the one who made all this possible. Thank you, Robert.

And then, Ginni. What I witnessed in Zurich, a scene that's playing out hundreds of times each week in dozens of cities around the world, was Ginni's doing much more than it was mine. She approved it, set the tone, stuck with it, and supported us for years without a word of doubt. As she led IBM's turnaround in the face of declining growth, she never lost faith in the possibilities that would be unleashed by change. Thank you, Ginni.

To my original team who risked everything and left their blood on the tracks of Change—Charlie, Karel, Adam, Pierre-Henri, Fahad, Melissa—and everyone else who appears in this book, thank you.

A special thanks to Doug Powell who, as you see in the book, was so instrumental in developing strategies that helped scale our success.

I worked so closely with six people who made my IBM life easier than it should have been. Thank you, Denise Reierson, my administrative assistant from the business process management days to the very end. Thank you, Danielle Jenkins, who kept me, and many others, out of finance jail for 12 years. Thank you, Joni Saylor, who to this day sets the standard for IBM designers through her style, grace, and intellect. Thank you also to Bill Grady—a third-generation IBMer!—and to Hal Wuertz and Mbiyimoh Ghogomu, all of whom carried on the rotational assignment Joni established as my designers-in-residence.

This book contains stories I've told countless times, but it took me three years of writing—and rewriting—to realize I didn't know how to tell the larger story. How many dozens of Chapter 1s did I write? I met Joanne Gordon, who introduced me to Alison Schwartz at Gotham Ghostwriters. Thank you both for your early encouragement to write the book, and for connecting me with my collaborator on this book, Noel Weyrich. It took just two days for Noel to figure out the book (and the title!), and over the past year he's been a great collaborative partner, writer, and editor. He not only unlocked the narrative arc but also drew out the all-important why behind every decision. Thank you, Noel. I could not have done this without you.

Thank you to the best PR team in the business, at Mark Fortier PR in New York. They understood the assignment from the first day we met.

Thank you to the thousands of IBM designers who, with your backbones of steel and 8-to-8 attitudes, did the heaviest lifting of all. I will be forever grateful for the time we spent together. I love you all.

And, finally, chapeau to the Knights of the Roundtable. You know who you are. Keep the flame lit.

About the Author

Phil Gilbert is best known for leading IBM's transformation as their General Manager of Design. After selling his third startup to IBM in 2010, Phil was asked by IBM in 2012 to use design thinking, coupled with agile, to update how IBM's teams worked. The transformation became the subject of a Harvard Business School case study, the documentary film *The Loop*, and feature articles in the *New York Times* and *Fortune Magazine*.

Phil's 45-year career spans startups, large corporations, and board memberships, where he has led organizations ranging from solo ventures to those with 400,000 employees.

In 2018 Phil was inducted into the New York Foundation for the Arts' Hall of Fame. In 2019, the State of Oklahoma (Phil's native state) named him an Oklahoma Creativity Ambassador for his achievements in the world of creative thinking and innovation.

Phil retired from full-time operational responsibilities at IBM in 2022 in order to focus on helping the next generation of entrepreneurs, business, and military leaders understand how to impact culture at scale, to improve innovation and team performance. Phil lives in Austin, Texas.

Index